Miniature Gardens

First published in 2014 by Cool Springs Press, an imprint of the Quayside Publishing Group, 400 First Avenue North, Suite 400, Minneapolis, MN 55401

Cool Springs Press titles are also available at discounts in bulk quantity for industrial or sales-promotional use. For details write to Special Sales Manager at Cool Springs Press, 400 First Avenue North, Suite 400, Minneapolis, MN 55401 USA. To find out more about our books, visit us online at www.coolspringspress.com.

Library of Congress Cataloging-in-Publication Data

Elzer-Peters, Katie.
   Miniature gardens : design & create miniature fairy gardens, dish gardens, terrariums and more-- indoors and out / Katie Elzer-Peters.
       pages cm
   Includes index.
   ISBN 978-1-59186-575-9 (sc)
   1. Gardens, Miniature. 2. Miniature plants. I. Title.

   SB433.5.E493 2014
   635--dc23

                         2013038735

ISBN: 978-1-59186-575-9

Group Publisher: Bryan Trandem
Editorial Director: Mark Johanson
Acquisitions Editor: Billie Brownell
Editor: Tracy Stanley
Assistant Managing Editor: Caitlin Fultz
Production Manager: Laura Hokkanen
Design Manager: Cindy Samargia Laun
Design & Layout: Simon Larkin
Cover Design: Mary Ann Smith

Cover: Thanks to Tonkadale Greenhouse, Minnetonka, MN; www.tonkadale.com
Cover photo by Paul Markert

Printed in China
10 9 8 7 6 5 4 3 2 1

Miniature Gardens

Design and Create Miniature Fairy Gardens,
Dish Gardens, Terrariums and More—Indoors and Out

KATIE ELZER-PETERS

COOL
SPRINGS
PRESS
Home and Garden Experts™

MINNEAPOLIS, MINNESOTA

For Mom, my "gardening angel."

ACKNOWLEDGMENTS

Many thanks to all of the people, businesses, and friends who helped me get this book together. Garden centers around the country, including Transplanted Garden, Lou's Flower World, The Plant Place, Allisonville Nursery, Succulent Gardens, Pender Pines, and Sullivan's Hardware all allowed me to take photos of anything I wanted whenever I wanted. To the WORLD'S GREATEST LIVING HAND MODELS, Susan Miller, Sharna Tolfree, and Joy Elzer, I appreciate your time and talents. Photography assistants Lexy Malone and Ashley Carr made the work of photo shoots in the heat and humidity much more bearable. Many thanks to Sharna for her creativity and artistry with project accessory design. To Francine Klimchak, who got the party started, and her chicken gardening friend Diane Jorge, I appreciate your help and generosity. My thanks to editors Billie Brownell and Tracy Stanley for your help and organization. Jerry Dockery—you know I couldn't get anything done without you, your truck, and Sugah and Lucy Too. Thank you to my friends and neighbors Sharon Nalley and Kelley Rodill for letting me steal mulch, sticks, and other assorted flotsam from your garden. I couldn't do any of this without my dad, Bob Elzer, and my husband, Joe Peters, who have to bear the emotional strain book writing brings with it. Tiffany Polli, I will always think of you when I see your beautiful photographs and succulent container gardens featured in this book. Robin Stockwell, you've taught me so much about succulents that I'm thrilled to share with others. Last but not least, thank you to all of my dear friends (not already mentioned above) who have helped me carry the load with all of my other work when I needed to clone myself or gave me a shoulder to lean on when I needed one: Jenny Peterson, Kim Sutton, Patty Davis, Barbara Bach, Lisa Schell, Jason Colclough, John and Amy Beausang, April Zilg, Susan Morrison, Rebecca Sweet, Laura Livengood, Kylee Baumlee, Barbara Fahs, Michael Nolan, Steve Asbell, Danielle Ernest, Chris McLaughlin, Brooke Foreman, and Shawna Coronado. And a very special thank you to Carol Michel and the Garden Fairies of May Dreams Gardens for their authentic stamp of fairy approval!

Contents

FOREWORD

Hello, garden fairies here.

We were gobsmacked to have been asked to write a foreword for a book about miniature gardens. We were so excited that we immediately called a meeting of all the garden fairies near and far to read the book and offer our opinions before turning it over to our scribe and most trusted garden fairy, Violet Greenpea Maydreams.

We garden fairies like how the book is organized. In the first part, Katie, the author, explains what a miniature garden is and what it is not, and writes about the importance of scale and design and the right plants so that the garden just looks right once it has been planted. She also tells how to care for the gardens, which we garden fairies think is of utmost importance because whether large or small, a garden that has not been cared for is one that we will leave faster than a rabbit can eat a row of green beans.

We garden fairies *love* that the book covers both indoor gardens as well as outdoor gardens. Don't think for one minute that we garden fairies wouldn't go inside in the winter if there were a good indoor garden to stay in. We would! We do!

But what really made us happiest was that Katie did not finish her miniature gardens by adding little plastic statues of garden fairies to all of them. We garden fairies believe in garden features like fountains, chairs, and arbors that are sized for a miniature garden. However, when people plant life-sized gardens, do they put life-sized people mannequins in those gardens? They do not. That would be ridiculous! We rest our case on why Katie's miniature gardens, which are like regular gardens, only smaller, are *just* the right size for anyone who enjoys creating something beautiful and living either for the outdoors or indoors.

We are garden fairies, and we put our stamp of approval on this book.
Yours truly,

Violet Greenpea Maydreams
Chief Scribe for the Garden Fairies at May Dreams Gardens, www.maydreamsgardens.com

What is the most fun about miniature gardening? The plants?
The accessories? It's impossible to decide. It's all fun!

INTRODUCTION

Miniature gardening is a way to garden, indoors and out, when space, time, or seasons are limited or when "regular" full-sized outdoor gardening isn't enough to fuel the fire of the imagination. With miniature gardening, you can create entire worlds in just a square foot or two of a container or a spot carved out in your big garden. It's like playing dollhouse but in an oasis of green instead of inside a wooden or plastic structure.

This type of gardening isn't limited to creating little worlds where a fairy or a small hobbit might find respite. It's also a way to enjoy plants (such as water plants or succulents) that require different conditions than your main garden can provide or to introduce variety to your landscape on a small and affordable scale.

Once you try it, you'll find yourself hooked. I was.

In the Beginning

I have always loved plants. I had a garden when I was six or seven. At the end of the season, my dad would dig up that year's asparagus fern so that I could grow it in a big terra cotta pot situated next to my west-facing bedroom window. I went to a lot of day camps when I was little. The highlight of one of them (who remembers which one now? not me) was when we made terrariums with gallon-and-a-half pickle jars. I'm not sure how long I had that terrarium, but I clearly remember sitting in the alcove of the school where the camp was being held, shoveling soil into the wide mouth of that jar.

Years later, I commandeered a fish bowl to make another terrarium. I used a clear glass plate from the restaurant where I worked as a lid for the terrarium. It sat in the area of my parents' house that was supposed to be a wet bar, but I had turned it into my "greenhouse." It had a sink, a counter, and big windows. Pity to waste that on a bar!

I grew all sorts of things in my little "greenhouse" until I went to college. Fast forward to many years later. I was in the middle of working on my first book (*Beginner's Illustrated Guide to Gardening*, Cool Springs Press). Instead of shooting photos in the hot blast-furnace atmosphere of my front yard, I went terrarium-crazy in the air-conditioned interior of my home. I planted small terrariums and Wardian cases and hanging terrariums. My husband thought I'd lost my mind. We had terrariums *all over the house*.

The peril of being a garden writer is that sometimes during the busy season you don't have enough time to actually *garden*. With miniature gardening, there's never a problem. Thirty seconds to water and a minute to clip some errant vines to prevent them from taking over, and you're done for the day. The rest of the time you can just admire your work. In a miniature garden or terrarium, you can get so much satisfaction, exercise so much control, and accomplish much more in a shorter amount of time than with any other type of gardening.

So What Is *Miniature* Gardening?

Miniature gardening (or mini-gardening), fairy gardening, terrarium-building, and aerium constructing are all just ways of making little landscapes or little scenes out of plants and, sometimes, accessories. In mini-gardening, you're telling a story, setting a stage, inviting intrigue and imagination to take over where the planting leaves off.

When you're finished planting your creation, you will have something other than just a collection of plants. You will have conjured a sense of possibility.

It's Different from Container Gardening

While you will plant many of your mini-gardens in containers, these little gardens aren't really container gardens the way you'd normally think of container gardens. You're not using plants as "thrillers," "fillers," and "spillers" to create a balanced look for pretty patio color. While mini-gardening you'll be repurposing plants that were previously annuals, perennials, or houseplants to serve as "trees" and "shrubs," using groundcovers as "grass," and finding the smallest, most dwarf version of your favorite flowering plants to add color to your mini-garden.

In the end, you'll have something that looks quite like your front yard or garden, only it will be smaller in diameter than the opening of a half–whiskey barrel.

Mini-Gardening Starts with Design

To make a miniature garden that looks like a small-scale landscape, you have to know a little bit about design. Design? What? Not *me*! It's a word that strikes fear in the hearts of many a gardener, but it need not. The same types of design principles that you use to create your full-sized garden will come in handy when you're planting your mini-garden. Chapter 1 goes into great detail about design. Here's a preview, though.

There are five key design areas that you'll learn about:

- Scale
- Contrast
- Repetition
- Focal point
- Theme

If you create your garden thinking only about those five principles, you'll be good to go. You will also find, I think, that you'll naturally employ these principles when creating a miniature garden, because the miniature garden will look so much better to your casual eye when you use them.

This garden demonstrates all of the design principles you'll learn about. Notice, in particular, the repetition of the contrasting chartreuse color of the miniature conifer dwarf Hinoki cypress, *Chamaecyparis obtusa* 'Golden Sprite', next to the white statue and the sedum growing in front of the miniature hosta.

For instance, when choosing plants, you'll find that you have to put a burgundy-leafed plant next to a light green-leafed plant, or some gravel, or a light-colored accessory; otherwise, it won't show up. That's the principle of contrast.

What all of the design principles really do is help you avoid ending up with a big blob of green in the container, as opposed to a miniature landscape design.

The Same as Container Gardening

Miniature gardening is the same as container gardening. Wait—didn't I just finish telling you that miniature gardening is *not* the same as container gardening? It is different in terms of the outcome of the garden, what you're hoping for in the finished product: a scene rather than a big riot of color.

Miniature gardening is the *same* as container gardening in terms of the factors you have to consider when selecting and combining plants. Because everything is planted relatively close together in a miniature garden, you have to plant "like with like." This refers to the conditions that plants in the mini-garden need in order to grow.

Like with like means:

- Sun plants with sun plants
- Shade plants with shade plants
- High-water-use plants with high-water-use plants
- Succulents and low-water-use plants with other low-water-use plants

One of the projects in the book is a miniature outdoor water garden. This incorporates plants that need wet soil, which is usually not present in a lot of gardens without intervention from the gardener. The plants used for the project all grow well in full to partial sun and need moist soil around their roots. They've thrived in the little "microclimate" I provided for them while other drought-lovers flourish in absurdly well-drained soil in the ground around them.

I enjoy miniature gardening because it lets me add my personality to the gardens. Here, I have a replica of my beloved purple BARK paddleboard and Kialoa paddle "floating" above my "Under the Sea" garden. A ceramic beagle (representing my dog Jack Daniels, who likes to paddle with me) stands on the board.

Mini-Gardening Sounds Complicated; Why Do I Want to Do It?

First of all, it really isn't that complicated. Once you start, you'll find yourself scouting for—and finding—plants, containers, accessories, and ideas everywhere you go. But the careful consideration and time needed to track down the right plants, containers, and "set pieces" is so worth it if you:

- Want to create a unique conversation piece
- Enjoy fun, hands-on projects
- Have limited time or space to garden
- Are mobility-challenged
- Want to grow plants that aren't well suited to your natural garden climate
- Live somewhere with long, hot summers or long, freezing winters
- Have kids or grandkids
- Want to try something different

Types of Miniature Gardening

You'll hear *miniature gardening* and *fairy gardening* discussed interchangeably. Technically, I guess they're about the same thing: creating tiny landscapes. The accessories and furniture are, for the most part, what turn a miniature garden into a landscape. A plant doesn't necessarily serve as a tree until a little bench is set underneath it (providing scale). Some people say that fairy gardens have to have little fairies in them, while others say that the garden must only be set up and look inviting to any fairies that might be flitting around.

Whether you add a fairy to the garden or not is entirely up to you. Your choice of plants, containers, and accessories will depend more on where you're planning to put the miniature garden than on whether a fairy will perch on one of the chairs or benches.

The projects in this book illustrate how to create some of the most popular types of miniature gardens. Reading about these and trying your hand at creating some of them will give you ideas for designing your own. The sky's the limit.

Indoor Miniature Gardens

Indoor miniature gardens are planted with houseplants or plants that can tolerate (or even thrive) in relatively low-light, indoor conditions. Containers for indoor miniature gardens are usually plastic, glass, or metal, and might be nestled inside another container that hides a drainage pan. Indoor miniature gardens can be placed outside during the summer but are indoors all winter.

Terrariums

A variation on the indoor miniature garden, terrariums are (usually) enclosed clear-glass containers planted with plants that like high humidity and lower light conditions. Terrariums do not have to be fully enclosed. Simply planting in a container with tall walls, such as a hurricane-style vase, elevates the humidity for the plants inside. Fully enclosed terrariums are self-sustaining ecosystems, requiring little, if any, extra water.

Aeriums

Think of an aerium as an open terrarium for air plants. The glass container helps elevate the humidity for the air plants, which contrary to common knowledge, actually do require some moisture to live. In general, aeriums are drier than terrariums, though, and are planted with different plants. They also require more frequent watering than terrariums that are fully enclosed.

Outdoor Miniature Gardens

The outdoor miniature gardens projects in this book describe how to create an outdoor miniature or fairy garden in a container. Most of the outdoor gardens will contain plants that are hardy to the area in which they are planted and will survive the winter in the container outside. Outdoor gardens can be brought in for a few days to serve as a centerpiece, but the plants in them are happier when they stay outside most of the time. Accessories for outdoor gardens need to be more durable, as well—resisting rust, corrosion, and water damage.

In-Situ Outdoor Miniature Gardens

You can plant a mini-garden *in situ* (Latin for "in position") in the middle of your regular full-sized garden using the same types of plants and accessories you'd gather for an outdoor miniature container garden. Because they stay in place, these gardens are planted mostly with hardy perennials or dwarf trees or shrubs, with some annuals thrown in for color. If you like to collect miniature conifers, an in-situ garden is a good choice.

What About Bonsai?

Where does bonsai fit into the miniature gardening trend? The art of bonsai involves training and pruning both the tops and the roots of trees to keep them miniature. Bonsai originated in China around 200 AD. The word **bonsai** means "planted in a container," and originated in Japan during the late 1800s.

To keep a bonsai tree alive for decades takes highly specialized care and attention, for which most people have neither the time nor the patience. The U.S. National Arboretum houses a collection of 150 bonsai, some of which are more than 350 years old. Some of the most interesting pieces in the collection are small bonsai forests containing several trees no taller than 2 or 3 feet.

Painstaking pruning and training keep these trees tiny but ensure that they grow to resemble the form of a mature tree many times the size of the bonsai form. Traditional bonsai involves much more than the plant itself. Stones, containers, and pruning shapes all have meanings in the world of bonsai. While you could put an accessory such as a bench under a bonsai tree, somehow that seems like it would disrupt the philosophical intent of bonsai.

Bonsai starts, available at some garden centers, do, however, make good plants for many miniature gardens—just be aware that eventually, without the root pruning, bonsai starts will get too large for the container and will have to be replaced.

A fairy garden in a 4-inch pot is small enough for a child's bedside table or bedroom windowsill but large enough to include a few fun accessories.

A "food crops" miniature garden at the San Francisco Flower and Garden Show.

A kid's miniature garden using recycled materials, including baby food jars and lids.

Mini-Gardening with Kids

If you have kids or grandkids, miniature gardening is one way to keep them occupied for hours. You can go different routes: make terrariums with recycled glass jars, make permanent fairy gardens that the kids can grow for the summer, or make temporary fairy "gardens" with items they collect around the yard.

A miniature garden doesn't have to be large for children to enjoy it. You can make one in a small pot, add a little animal or accessory, and still have a pint-sized scene that a child can enjoy tending. (By making a smaller garden with fewer plants, they're also more likely to have better luck maintaining it.)

The San Francisco Flower and Garden Show has a miniature garden contest for kids. Individuals and classrooms or clubs compete. They seem to always come up with fascinating designs and themes, from "crop gardens" demonstrating agricultural products in different countries, to bee gardens, to miniature "vegetable" gardens.

Fairy gardening doesn't have to be fancy to be fun, but it will tickle the fancy of almost all children, boys and girls, and ignite their imaginations.

Speaking of Imagination

Everything from here on will teach you the basics of creating miniature gardens and fairy gardens to grow indoors or out. There are some projects, tips, hints, and lots of photos to inspire you.

Once you have the basics down, use your imagination to create enchanting gardens that only *you* can dream up.

Part 1
MINIATURE GARDENING BASICS

Part 1 of this book will teach you the fundamentals you need to understand in order to complete the projects in Part 2. Learn how to:

- Design a miniature garden
- Select the right plants
- Choose an appropriate container
- Find accessories
- Care for the miniature garden

Remember, these basics are just a starting point for miniature gardening. Use your imagination to create your own little worlds.

When placing accessories, always look at the garden from the potential visitor's point of view.

Chapter 1
DESIGN

A lot of gardeners freeze when they think about design: "Design is for professionals, not for me!" Designing a garden (large or small) is less complicated than it seems. Once you learn a few basic tips, you'll feel like a pro in no time. You'll also find yourself looking at gardens differently—noticing elements of design and learning things that you can apply to your own projects.

But wait—do you really need to understand design to plant a miniature garden? Yes, you really do. If you don't, you'll end up with a big mess in a small pot without any structure or interest (not that anyone's going to be judging your creation). You'll be happier with it if you think about the plantings. Remember, we're going for small-scale landscapes here. You'll use houseplants, annuals, and perennials as "trees," "shrubs," and "groundcovers" to create a miniature landscape into which you can place accessories that turn the landscape into a true miniature world.

The principles you're going to learn come straight from "regular" gardening and landscaping. We're just going to apply them to smaller-scale landscapes.

Design turns a random collection of plants and stuff into a little landscape or scene.

Scale

More important than almost anything else in miniature garden design, the idea of scale is what creates the miniature world. In miniature gardening, scale is the relationship of the plants to each other and to the accessories, in terms of size. A "tree" in the miniature garden landscape is only a tree because it is as tall, in proportion, to the fairy house or garden bench as a large tree would be to a regular-sized house or garden bench.

You've probably heard the term *scale model*, which refers to a copy of something (a building, an airplane, a model train) in which details on the copy are reproduced in the same relative proportions as they appear on the original. Scientific and architectural scale models have fixed proportions such as 1:8, 1:16, or 1:64. In a 1:8 model, 1 inch on the model equals 64 inches on the object being copied.

In miniature gardening, you're gardening to scale, so you want the plants, trees, and accessories to be in proportion to one another, but you don't necessarily have to measure to a precise scale like you would for a model train set or architectural model. You can, for the most part, eyeball it. You'll know if something looks "off."

In this large miniature garden, a small ficus plant serves as the "tree" next to the fairy house. A *Hosta* 'Blue Mouse Ears' is a large shrub. Ferns also grow along the side of the house as "shrubs." The groundcover is *Pilea* 'Aquamarine'.

Scale: Pairing Accessories with Each Other

You can find miniature gardening accessories everywhere (particularly online) and in all shapes, sizes, and styles. After you choose a style (more on that in Chapter 3), you can start finding accessories to use together. The example pictures were created with accessories for a fairly ornate Victorian-style garden: wrought-iron chairs, concrete benches, large garden containers, a fountain, and a pergola. But just because the *style* of the accessories matches doesn't mean that the *scale* matches. Take a look.

Out of Scale

This photo shows a concrete bench and a fountain. The fountain is much too small to be paired with the bench, unless the fountain was supposed to be a tabletop fountain. In that case, the container and rest of the landscape are too small to accommodate both accessories. (You'd also need a table to put that tabletop fountain on.)

Good to Grow

This picture shows the same concrete bench with a "large" planting urn. (It's large in the sense that it looks "in proportion" to the bench, functioning as a big accent planter.)

Out of Scale

Here, the bench is paired with the pergola, and it looks kind of ridiculous. The bench is much too large to complement the scale of the pergola.

Good to Grow

In this picture, the too-large bench has been replaced with a smaller chair that fits with the size of the pergola. You could fit two of the smaller chairs in the pergola. To make the same pergola look even bigger, you could accessorize with two even smaller chairs.

Good to Grow

In this miniature garden, the large(er) seashells at the base of the screw pine "tree" are used more for accents. They're not meant to be in-scale with the garden. You could pretend that they're big hermit crabs or horseshoe crabs washed ashore. The little shells in the bucket, however, are to scale. The shells fit in the bucket, and the bucket looks like it matches the chair, in terms of size. You wouldn't be surprised to be walking along the beach, happening upon this little scene. Now, if the bucket was the size of the chair that would look odd. A child's fantasy, maybe: a beach bucket the size of a tent. You don't see that every day.

Scale: Pairing Accessories with Plants

The magic with miniature gardens happens in the relationship between plants and accessories. You can play all kinds of tricks of perspective when you pair the same plants with different sizes of accessories. It isn't necessarily possible to end up with the wrong scale of plants, unless you use a plant that doesn't perform the function you want it to. That function is created by the difference in size between the plant and the accessory.

Same Furniture—Different Plants—Different "Story"

In these two miniature gardens (bottom photos), the bistro table and chairs are used for different effects when the plants are changed. The garden in the blue container with the American flag, bicycle, and birdhouse is planted with a large plant serving as a "tree," providing shade for the table and chairs. Polka dot plants (pink and green and white and green) and a fern serve as smaller "shrubs." An oak-leaved ficus is a groundcover. The garden has a more casual feel, with the addition of the "tree." The scene depicts what could be a front yard or backyard in a small town.

The gardens are about the same size, as is the furniture. Illusions! The same furniture looks smaller when placed next to bigger plants. That's one way that scale works in the miniature garden.

The garden without the large tree, in the orange terra cotta pot, has a more formal and ornate feel. The plants are smaller, and without a large specimen tree, the focus remains squarely on the furniture. Because the furniture is larger in relation to the plants in the terra cotta pot, the garden or "scene" looks smaller. This garden depicts more of a patio scene set for tea than a whole backyard as shown in the blue container on the right.

In this photo (left), the dinosaur is only about 2½ inches long from nose to tail and about ¾ inch tall. Nestled in among small ferns and a croton, it looks like it's tromping through a jungle of plants. If you swapped this dinosaur for one that was two or three times as big (something you might see at a toy store), all of a sudden the plants would look smaller and the dinosaur would look like he's out for a casual stroll on the prehistoric plain instead of walking through the rainforest.

The dinosaur in this terrarium illustrates the same principle of accessory size to plant size.

Scale

Matching structures to furniture: Make sure that a chair or wheelbarrow is smaller than a house.

Matching accessories to furniture: Dishes should look like they belong on a table. For example: a cup should not be as big as an entire picnic table. The same goes for garden tools and potting benches as well as "hanging baskets" and pergolas.

Incorporating animals: A bunny rabbit or cat shouldn't be as big as a chair. Unless *your* cat is as big as a patio chair.

A small screw pine becomes a large "tree" in this beach garden. *Sempervivum* (behind the beach chair) stand in for the yuccas you often see growing at the beach. *Haworthia* plants (on the right side of the garden) imitate large agaves that grow along beach dunes.

What makes this perennial border at Longwood Gardens in Kennett Square, Pennsylvania, so beautiful? The contrast. There are contrasting textures (ferny leaves contrast with large, thick leaves), contrasting colors (pink and purple, chartreuse and burgundy), and contrasting forms (mounded plants and spiky plants).

Contrast

The next most important aspect of miniature garden design to master after scale is the idea of contrast: differences between the elements in the garden. This applies to regular full-sized landscaping as well as miniature gardening. In fact, you can learn a lot about contrast from looking at "big plants" and applying your observations when you pick out the "little plants."

Why Is Contrast So Important?

It's possible that contrast is even more important in a miniature garden than in a full-sized landscape because everything in it is so small. If it all looks the same—is the same color, same shape, has the same-sized leaves—the miniature garden will just look like a blob.

The Big Three: Color, Form, and Texture

You can create contrast in the garden when you concentrate on selecting plants with differing color, form, and texture.

Contrasting Color

If design makes people nervous, color is probably the part people worry about the most. The main thing about color combinations is that if you like the way two plants look side by side, that's all that matters. Don't be afraid to try something unusual. That's what will make your plantings really stand out.

Creating Contrast

Try these contrasting combinations:

- Big leaves with small leaves
- Textured leaves with smooth leaves
- Cool-colored foliage with warm-colored foliage
- Round leaves (hosta) with lance-shaped or long, skinny leaves (mondo grass)
- Light-colored leaves with dark-colored leaves
- Light-colored furniture with dark-colored plants
- Light-colored plants with dark-colored furniture

The main contrast in this miniature garden is the bright white furniture against dark green plant leaves.

It's not just plants you have to think about when creating contrast in the garden. Accessories should contrast with their backgrounds (in this case, a brown cat on gray gravel) if you want the accessories to stand out.

I like this color combination because a bit of the purple from the *Angelonia* flowers also appears in the stems of the chartreuse-leafed coleus. Purple and chartreuse are a surefire contrasting color scheme for the garden.

This color combination is pretty, if fairly standard. All three plants are "warm colors" (shades of red, orange, and yellow).

In this grouping, the rust-colored coleus from the previous grouping has been switched with a silver-colored *Plectranthus*. POW! It really pops. The silver is a cool color that contrasts with the warmer colors of the ornamental grass and petunias.

Sometimes miniature garden color contrasts are more subdued, simply because you'll find yourself working more with foliage plants than flowers.

In this garden (above), the purple and chartreuse contrast is achieved with *Ajuga* 'Chocolate Chips' (below the chair on the right) and *Laurentia* (the light-colored groundcover plant). I didn't plant the *Ajuga* next to the dark-green-leafed mondo grass, as it would have just disappeared and blended with the similarly dark-leafed mondo grass. Contrast is what allows you to see different plants growing in such a small space.

Variegation: Built-in Contrast

The most common variegation is two-toned green-and-white plants. The white is due to lack of chlorophyll (pigment that reflects green light, among other things) in certain areas of the plant. When you use these plants, you have built-in contrast.

Many miniature garden plants, particularly houseplants, are available in variegated forms.

Contrasting Form

Contrasting form can be one of the trickiest design elements to achieve in miniature garden design because many of the plants (especially small houseplants and terrarium plants) have a similar form: Many are mounding in habit. To add interest to the garden, look for plants with long, thin leaves and a vertical growth habit, or a plant with a trailing growth habit, instead of a "roundy-moundy" habit.

This garden shows *Penstemon* (back) and lady's mantle (front). The *Penstemon* has a strong vertical growth habit, while the lady's mantle has a lower, mounding growth form.

This picture shows two different plants for the miniature garden with different growth forms. *Hosta* 'Blue Mouse Ears' (left) has a compact, mounding form. *Euphorbia* 'Diamond Frost' (right) has a rambling, flopping, reaching growth form.

Contrasting Texture

It's easy to confuse form with texture. They're not the same thing. Leaf shapes and characteristics are what offer texture in most miniature garden plants.

This "regular-sized" garden combination *Hakonechloa* (ornamental grass on the left) and hosta (right) shows two plants with similar forms (mounding), but different textures. (They also have good contrasting colors in their leaves.) The skinny leaves of the grass contrast nicely with the wide leaves of the hosta.

In full-sized gardens, hosta and ferns are often planted together for contrast. They also both have mounding habits. The ferns have highly dissected (incised) leaves, which contrast with the large, smooth hosta leaves.

Here's an example of texture contrast in miniature garden plants. Both of these ferns have relatively upright growing habits. The one on the right has smaller, more ruffled leaves that contrast with the larger, smoother leaves of the fern on the left.

The Tennis Court garden at Chanticleer Gardens in Wayne, Pennsylvania.

Repetition

The Tennis Court garden at Chanticleer Gardens in Wayne, Pennsylvania, is one of the most beautiful gardens I've ever seen. They have the color, form, and texture contrast concept down pat. It's a textbook example of how to use those design concepts to create an interesting garden that encourages you to keep looking, rather than settling in one fixed spot.

If you look closely at this picture, though, you'll notice something else: repetition. Colors, forms, and textures are repeated throughout the garden. The color chartreuse is a motif in this garden. It winds through the beds like a river. To repeat something like color, you don't have to use the same plants everywhere (though in a miniature garden, that is the easiest way to do it without cluttering up the container). You can see that they've used at least three different plants with chartreuse leaves to keep the color going throughout the garden. Silver is another color that's repeated, though in different plants with differing heights, textures, or growth forms.

How do you use repetition in the mini-garden? There are three easy ways to do it.

Choose Plants that "Talk to Each Other"

That means plants that have a similar color or colors running through each of the plants. Here's an example of that in a "large" container garden (below, left).

You could also achieve this effect with texture by using a large plant and a small plant or plants, each with grassy-type leaves.

Burgundy or chartreuse appear in each of the plants in this large container planting. The repetition between plants unifies the look.

Here's an example with "mini" plants. Chartreuse green is present in the *Selaginella* (top left) and croton (bottom center). Dark green is present in the leaves of the croton and the polka dot plant (top right).

Repeat a Color with Accessories

Can't find enough color in the plants? Select accessories that will repeat one of your accent colors. In this miniature garden, the red watering can and red wheelbarrow repeat the red of the zinnias.

Repeat a Plant

It's easiest to repeat groundcovers or "shrubs," simply because they're small. In this miniature garden, the white polka dot plant hops over the patio and is planted on the other side of the dining set to encourage a viewer's eye to move around and not just settle on one group of plants.

Focal Point

If you've ever planted a container garden, you've probably heard about using "thrillers, fillers, and spillers." A thriller is the biggest, most interesting plant specimen in the container. Usually, unless it is a really large container (think parking lot–sized urn), you only have one thriller. The spillers trail over the edge of the pot, and the filler fills in and unifies the space between the thriller and the spiller. In a sense, the thriller is the focal point of the container, the plant you notice the most.

Use the same idea with a miniature garden. One really spectacular plant or accessory is usually enough. The beach garden is a good example of this. The screw pine is the focal point. All of the other plants and accessories are smaller and play supporting roles. In the Victorian garden, the table and chairs are the focal point, or dominant item, in the garden. If you have too many large plants or accessories in one container there's no point for the eye to rest on.

But wait: Didn't I just say that repetition keeps the eye from fixing on a specific point and staying there? Yes, but it's okay to give the eyes a break. Repetition in smaller accessories or plants and repetition in colors can actually unify the garden. Too many big objects in a small garden is just messy, though. Repetition helps the garden become more than just a collection of plants. It turns the garden into a designed landscape.

Larger gardens can handle more than one focal point. In a bigger miniature garden you can create even smaller scenes within the mini-garden. In this outdoor miniature garden (top right), the fairy house is the main focal point, but there's also a little garden bench catty-corner to the house (bottom right), a secondary "scene." A birdbath and a rabbit complete the vignette.

Focal Point: Fairy's-Eye
When placing accessories, kneel down and look at the garden from a fairy's-eye view. What would they see if they sat in the little chairs or perched on one of the branches, or walked out the door of their little fairy house? This gazing ball, when moved to the end of the pathway opposite the table and chairs, provides a nice focal point from the fairy's point of view.

The fairy house is the main focal point of this miniature garden.

The small bench is a secondary focal point within the same garden.

Theme

A garden's theme will influence plant, container, and accessory choices—all of which are elaborated upon in subsequent chapters. Theme is part of design because without a theme, a miniature garden can look like a bunch of random trinkets dropped into a container garden. There's no landscape to provide a backdrop for accessories. Without contrasting color, form, and texture, or the application of the principle of scale, you can't carry through a theme and make it look realistic.

Most of the projects in this book have a theme. There's a beach garden, Grandma's Garden, a Wild Wild West Garden, and a woodland garden, among others. The accessories are what carry most themes to their full realization, but plants also influence how successful a theme is. Succulents look ridiculous in woodland gardens, and a hosta would be completely out of place in an "under the sea" garden.

Accessories inspired the theme for the Wild Wild West Garden. The turquoise blue patio set looks right at home among *Tillandsia* "sagebrush," aloes, hens and chickens, and jade plants.

Plants provided the inspiration for this garden's theme. The miniature conifers were too cute to pass up. Paired with "concrete" and "marble" statues, they look like majestic full-sized specimens in a botanical garden—one that fits on an outdoor table.

A succulent dish garden has been finished with some blue tumbled glass mulch. Even without accessories, it's complete.

A succulent dish garden with some Asian-themed accessories. The accessories turn this creation into a miniature landscape.

Sometimes plants *are* the theme. Miniature water gardens and succulent dish gardens are mini-gardens that look 100 percent complete without extra furniture or accessories.

Understanding the basics of design will help you select the right plants, containers, and accessories to achieve the look you're going for, whether its an under-the-sea scuba setting or a woodland hideaway.

Chapter 2
PLANTS

While the accessories in miniature gardening are fun, we are, after all, *gardening*, so before thinking about patio furniture and miniature fountains, we have to think about the garden.

Once you start creating miniature gardens, you'll look at every plant with a new set of eyes. "Would this make a good 'tree' in my miniature garden?" you'll ask yourself. "Would this little vine climb up the pergola I bought or will it take over everything?" You'll read plant tags more critically and try to determine whether something that's in a small pot will actually stay small or grow slowly enough that it can stay in place for a year or two.

True miniature plants keep their diminutive size for many years without the need for pruning.

Plant Shopping

All of the projects in this book include a photo of the plants selected for the project. Notice that I said "selected" rather than "used." Often you'll have leftover plants, unless you carefully assembled all of the plants and the accessories you plan to use while you are still at the garden center. Sometimes you'll realize that one or two additional plants that you didn't purchase would complete the look, and you'll end up having to go back to the nursery.

The projects in this book are meant to be inspiration to guide you to create your own versions; don't worry about matching the plant lists exactly. The plants used will work for each project theme, but they aren't the *only* plants you can use for each type of theme. You might have different choices available for succulents or tiny houseplants. Not to worry. As long as you pay attention to the following items when selecting the plants for your miniature garden, you'll be in good shape:

- Plants' growth rate
- Garden type the plants will go in (indoor or outdoor)
- Landscape function of the plants
- Plant needs (light and water)

When shopping for small perennials or groundcovers, look for plants that can be split once removed from the container. This will allow you to use the plants in smaller clumps and will get you more bang for the buck. (Hint: if a plant has only one stem meeting the soil line, it can't be split.)

To avoid ending up with extra plants or a big hole in the miniature garden design, assemble your mini-garden at the garden center (you can leave the plants in the pots).

Branded Plants: Love 'em or Leave 'em?

Walk into a garden center and you're likely to find branded plants. Proven Winners is a popular brand of full-sized plants that most gardeners have seen at their local garden centers. They stand out, particularly, because of their white pots.

Stepables is a branded plant line of groundcovers and small plants in purple pots with tags shaped like feet. These are low-growing plants, mostly with small leaves, that can be suitable for miniature gardens.

A new line of branded plants, Fairy Flowers, has been selected as a collection of plants with small leaves, slow growth habits, or that respond well to trimming to maintain size. An important note about these plants is some require more maintenance than others. Just because a plant is branded as a fairy garden plant or has small leaves does not mean it won't take over the garden.

Stepables are groundcovers and can grow fast. While their small leaves make them suitable, in terms of scale, for miniature gardens, their quick growth rate can make them monsters in small pots before the end of the season.

A fairy garden planted with groundcovers will become overgrown without proper maintenance. There are accessories in this garden, such as an arbor and a watering can, but they've been overtaken by plants.

Each Fairy Flowers plant has a story that goes along with the fairy associated with the plant.

Table ferns are popular plants for indoor miniature gardens and terrariums. Look for plants in 1-inch pots.

Groundcovers can be annuals (such as maidenhair fern or wirevine) or perennials (such as Corsican mint or blue star creeper).

Plant Types

There are many ways to classify the plants used for miniature gardens. Before we get to the characteristics that will affect how you combine plants in a miniature garden, here's a crash course on types of plants you'll find while shopping.

Annuals

Annual flowers and foliage such as calibrachoa (million bells) and coleus are tropical in origin and only live for one season outside. You can use annual plants for color in the garden, but be aware that you'll have to replace them from season to season. For the most part, annuals do best when growing in outdoor miniature gardens, but you can experiment with them for indoor gardens.

Abutilon, or flowering maple, is an annual that looks like a little tree. Its flowers look like little fairy hats. Even though it will only last for one season, it's too cute to pass up.

USDA Plant Hardiness Zone Map

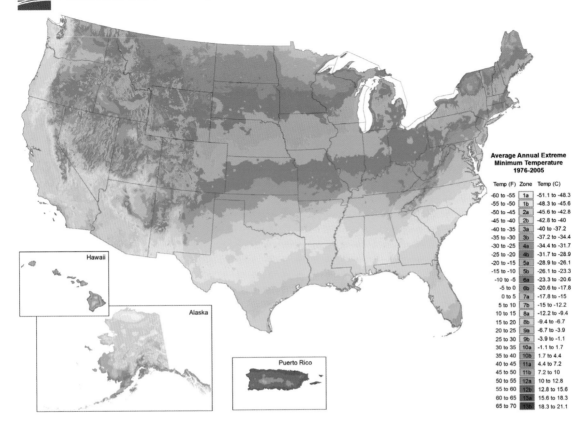

Temp (F)	Zone	Temp (C)
-60 to -55	1a	-51.1 to -48.3
-55 to -50	1b	-48.3 to -45.6
-50 to -45	2a	-45.6 to -42.8
-45 to -40	2b	-42.8 to -40
-40 to -35	3a	-40 to -37.2
-35 to -30	3b	-37.2 to -34.4
-30 to -25	4a	-34.4 to -31.7
-25 to -20	4b	-31.7 to -28.9
-20 to -15	5a	-28.9 to -26.1
-15 to -10	5b	-26.1 to -23.3
-10 to -5	6a	-23.3 to -20.6
-5 to 0	6b	-20.6 to -17.8
0 to 5	7a	-17.8 to -15
5 to 10	7b	-15 to -12.2
10 to 15	8a	-12.2 to -9.4
15 to 20	8b	-9.4 to -6.7
20 to 25	9a	-6.7 to -3.9
25 to 30	9b	-3.9 to -1.1
30 to 35	10a	-1.1 to 1.7
35 to 40	10b	1.7 to 4.4
40 to 45	11a	4.4 to 7.2
45 to 50	11b	7.2 to 10
50 to 55	12a	10 to 12.8
55 to 60	12b	12.8 to 15.6
60 to 65	13a	15.6 to 18.3
65 to 70	13b	18.3 to 21.1

Average Annual Extreme Minimum Temperature 1976-2005

The U.S. Department of Agriculture Hardiness Zone map indicates average annual minimum temperatures in areas of the United States. Plant tags for perennials, trees, and shrubs usually list hardiness zones, which are an indication of the plant's ability to withstand cold, not to tolerate heat. *USDA Plant Hardiness Zone Map, 2012. Agricultural Research Service, U.S. Department of Agriculture. Accessed from http://planthardiness.ars.usda.gov.*

Perennials

Perennials are the largest group of plants to select from for miniature gardens. They grow best in outdoor gardens, but you have to select varieties that are hardy in your area (will survive the coldest temperatures of winter) for them to come back from year to year. Perennials planted in containers usually give up one hardiness zone. If a perennial is marked as hardy to zone 5, if it's planted in a container, it will most likely only be hardy to zone 6 temperatures.

Miniature hostas, dwarf mondo grass, *Sedum*, and blue star creeper are popular perennials for miniature gardens. Look for perennials with small leaves and a low-growth habit for use as groundcovers or "shrubs." Perennials with larger leaves and growth habits can serve as "trees" in the miniature garden.

True large-garden groundcovers are perennials, but watch out for them. They grow fast (hence the name groundcovers) and can take over a miniature garden quickly. If you like to tinker with your garden, however, groundcovers are great because their fast growth gives you something to trim.

Dwarf mondo grass is a perennial groundcover in a large garden but can function as an ornamental grass or shrub in a miniature garden.

47

Sempervivum spp., also known as "hens and chicks," is a commonly available cold-hardy succulent. Within that plant group cold tolerance varies, so check the plant tags if you plan to leave them outdoors.

Succulents

Succulents are plants with fleshy leaves that hold water. Most succulents thrive in partial to full sun. You'll find some succulents in the perennials area of your garden center. Use those for outdoor gardens. There are many succulents hardy only in zones 8 to 10 that can be used in indoor mini-gardens. When choosing succulents for indoor gardens, select those that can deal with lower light levels. Also, when possible, move your indoor succulent garden outdoors for the summer.

Air Plants

Air plants are bromeliads in the *Tillandsia* group. Spanish moss is also part of this group. While Spanish moss can be dried and will retain its shape and general silvery color, other air plants don't dry well, and they do need to be watered. You can mist them a few times a week. (They can also be soaked in water, but that isn't always practical if they're glued or wired to something.)

Air plants will color up when they get ready to bloom. This air plant has just finished blooming.

After air plants bloom, the main plant dies and "pups" or babies will start growing from around the base of the big plant. Once the big plant is fully dead, you can clip it off and leave the baby.

Air plants come in a variety of colors, shapes, and sizes.

Houseplants

Many garden centers now have a section of the store labeled "Teeny Tiny Plants" in which the plants can be found in 1-inch pots. Most of these are indoor plants from tropical or extremely temperate regions (without hard freezes during the year). Some garden centers will mix succulents and houseplants together in displays, but you can't mix them together in a container. (More about that later in this chapter.) Houseplants are best suited for indoor miniature gardens and terrariums. Not all houseplants like the humid conditions provided by a terrarium, though, so do your research before enclosing plants in a sealed environment.

"Tiny plants" in 1-inch pots.

Juniperus horizontalis 'Pancake' is a low-spreading variety of the common creeping juniper. Its mature height is 1 inch tall by 2 feet wide at ten years.

Dwarf Conifers

Dwarf and miniature conifers are slow-growing, small-statured varieties of full-sized plants. They are not the same as bonsai starts. These small trees and shrubs are true minis that will stay small (though they do grow) without root pruning.

While adorable, they can be difficult to grow. They don't thrive in either very hot or very cold conditions. They will, however, when happy, grow in the same container for up to ten years. If you want a true miniature garden that can stay in the same container without repotting for years and years, dwarf conifers are worth a try. Unlike perennials that die back in the winter, these (mostly) evergreen plants provide interest year-round.

Bonsai Starts

Bonsai starts are seedlings of full-sized plants (mostly trees). While these plants are small, they don't necessarily grow slowly or stay small as dwarf and miniature plants do. Bonsai are kept small by pruning the roots and the top of the plant. Using a bonsai in a miniature garden means you'll occasionally have to dig up the plant to prune the roots in order to keep it small—unlike true dwarf or mini-plants.

Even if a garden center has an area marked fairy gardening or miniature gardening, make sure that you spend time outside of this special section looking for plants. There is no rule that you have to use only tiny plants in your gardens, or that you can't plant a cool coleus as a "tree."

Combining Plants in Mini-Gardens

These are the factors that you need to consider when selecting plants to grow together in a miniature garden.

Growth Rate

Just because a plant is in a small pot doesn't mean it will stay small. Many perennials and most annuals grow too fast or too big to stay long in a miniature garden or fairy garden. That doesn't mean you can't use them; you just need to be aware that you'll have to spend more time tending to your miniature garden (trimming the plants) and you'll have to replace the faster-growing plants with another plant sooner rather than later.

Dwarf vs. Miniature

Dwarf plants grow slowly, but can still reach a fairly large size, while true miniature plants stay small. The distinction is more in the eye of the beholder, but you'll have to count on switching out a plant marked as "dwarf" sooner than a miniature. For example, *Hosta* 'Blue Mouse Ears' never gets taller than 6 inches or so, but a dwarf Alberta spruce will eventually grow from a 12-inch plant to a 6-foot plant. It might take twenty years to get that big, but it will get bigger.

This dwarf conifer, *Chamecyparis obtusa* 'Golden Sprite', is growing in a 4-inch pot. It will reach a mature size of 4 inches tall by 12 inches wide in ten years. Is it a dwarf or a miniature? A dwarf conifer is any conifer that grows 1 to 6 inches in a single year. A miniature conifer is any conifer that grows less than 1 inch in a single year. This one's a miniature.

Garden Type

Are you planting an outdoor container garden, an outdoor in situ garden, a terrarium, or an indoor miniature garden? Where you will use the plants makes a difference. Use outdoor plants that are hardy in your area for the bones of an outdoor in situ garden. (You can pop annuals in and out for color if you want.) If you're planting a terrarium, you need a plant that can tolerate high humidity. Right plant, right place still applies for miniature gardening.

When possible, take your container when you shop for plants. Some tiny plants are too big for some containers. This picture shows a variegated ficus that, while small, is still too tall for the container selected for this terrarium project.

Landscape Function

You'll be using these plants to create a miniature landscape. That means variety is key. You need plants that can be groundcovers, plants that can be shrubs, plants that can be trees, and, sometimes, vining plants. While shopping, think about how you're going to use the plants. You might even position them and arrange them as you would in your planned miniature garden so that you know you're getting the right variety and the right scale for your intended project.

This miniature gardener is holding a potential "tree" next to the chicken coop she'll use in her miniature garden to check the size of the plant in relation to the accessory.

Plant Needs

Remember to plant "like with like." That means to plant sun-loving, water-loving plants with others that like the same conditions. Ditto for low-water succulents or shade plants. Just because plants aesthetically match each other doesn't mean they'll love growing together.

More about individual plants for miniature gardening, including photos, can be found in Part 3.

Humidity-loving houseplants grow well in enclosed terrariums.

(Above) Succulents should be planted together, as they are all low-water plants (in comparison to other plants). (Opposite) Once you start making mini-gardens, your patio or porch might or might not start to look like this porch, which might or might not be my porch. It is difficult to stop collecting.

Succulent Terrariums
Is there such a thing as a succulent terrarium? There is, and you'll see them all over the place. You'll notice that succulent terrariums are open, rather than fully enclosed, to allow air circulation. You have to be extremely careful not to overwater succulent terrariums. Water doesn't evaporate as fast out of these containers, and plants can quickly rot.

Look beyond the ordinary for miniature garden containers. This award-winning garden from Tiffany Polli is part miniature garden, part container garden, all adorable. Planted with succulents, including string of pearls for the "tea" coming out of the teapot, it's well suited for indoor locations with bright light. *Planting design and photo by Tiffany Polli*

Chapter 3
CONTAINERS

In miniature gardening, the container can either add to the theme or take away from it. The container can ensure the longevity of your planting design or cause you to have to replant before you're ready. Choosing the right container for your mini-garden or terrarium is as important as choosing the plants and accessories.

The ideal miniature garden container will:
- Enhance the theme
- Stand up to the conditions of the environment where the finished garden will sit
- Be large enough and deep enough for the plants it will contain

There are some containers that are better suited for indoor mini-gardens than outdoor gardens and vice versa. Terrarium containers have to have clear walls and a clear top in order to allow light to reach the plants.

On the following pages you'll find many tips for choosing the right container for your miniature garden.

Think About Drainage

Any container that is going to be used indoors that has drainage holes in it will require some sort of watertight tray underneath it. You can buy inexpensive clear plastic trays at garden centers. You can also use a decorative plate or platter. The important thing that the tray must do is protect your furniture from water.

This container from supplier Fairy Gardening is a square plastic box with drainage holes and a drain tray (not visible under the box). You can get various decorative boxes or fences to put the container in or to put around the container.

Drainage is important, and indoor containers can suffer when they don't have drainage holes. I selected this container for the beach garden because the wood on the outside looked beachy—like driftwood or a beach fence—but the container had no drainage. I grabbed an inexpensive plastic tray and poked holes in the bottom and put that inside the container. If the beach gets soggy, I can always pull it (albeit gently, and with help) out of the container.

A container without drainage holes requires rocks in the bottom or a container within the container that you can poke drainage holes in.

This container extends the theme of the garden inside it.

Water bowls make good containers for planting. Before planting, have the garden center drill a hole in the bottom.

Carry a Theme

The container can add to or detract from the overall theme of a mini-garden. If you can, it's nice to select a container that will help carry out the theme, as in the case of the Garden at the Beach.

Water bowls with a hole drilled in the bottom make great containers for outdoor miniature gardens. They're a bit thick and heavy for indoor gardens. Choose a color that complements your accessories and plants and use color in a container to your advantage. Many of the plants suitable for mini-gardens are mostly varying shades of green. A container is a great way to add some color to the design.

A cute fish container adds whimsy to this miniature garden.

The blue container enhances this backyard scene. It adds a nice patriotic flair with the flag, red bicycle, and white patio furniture.

Sometimes the container is as much a part of the garden as the plants. In the case of the teapot garden on page 58, the container makes the garden. This fish container (above, right) turns into a miniature underwater garden; the plants look like coral or seaweed, enhancing the effect of the fish container.

Consider the End-Use of the Container

The location in which you're planning to display the garden affects container selection as much as plant selection. A large container will be heavy when filled with plants and soil. Choose a big piece of pottery for containers that will stay put.

Durable pottery, terra cotta, or plastic containers hold up well outside, but repurposed items such as cigar boxes and many wooden containers are better suited for indoor use.

This fairy fountain should be planted with plants suitable for covered patio gardens and indoor gardens. The electrical system for the fountain makes it impractical for outdoor gardens.

Hypertufa containers are popular for miniature gardens because they drain well and aren't heavy (in comparison to full concrete pots). They're made from concrete and peat moss mixed together.

Hypertufa containers are popular for miniature gardens. You can actually make your own pots or get them from the garden center. These pots, unless planted with low-water-use succulents, are best for outside. They are porous and drain freely from all sides of the container, making them a messy choice for indoor plantings.

This hypertufa pot complements the plants and accessories inside it. It's heavy when planted, though, and should find a permanent home outdoors once the project is finished.

Let the Plants Shine

You can choose containers that further a garden's theme or containers that just hang in the background. The most obvious choices for neutral containers are round or square terra cotta pots. If you're planting succulents, azalea-style pots (which are shallower) work well.

This terra cotta pot is 12 inches in diameter and 6 inches deep. It's perfect for succulents.

Because the container isn't flashy, your attention easily focuses on the plants in this Under the Sea garden.

If you're planting a large outdoor garden, a shallow copper bowl makes a good unobtrusive container with plenty of room for lots of plants and accessories. If you wanted to plant a jumbo-sized outdoor mini-garden, you could use a copper fire bowl and stand. When using a container without external drainage, add rocks to the bottom of the container. If a big rainstorm is forecast, you might consider covering the garden with a tarp so that it does not become overly full of water.

This copper bowl sits on a short wrought-iron stand.

Terrarium containers run from everyday (Ball jars) to fancy (blown glass hanging terrarium containers like the one on the far left of the photo).

Terrarium Containers

Terrarium containers are usually all glass, though if most of the container is clear glass, part of it can be opaque—usually the bottom or the top.

While most people think of a terrarium as a wholly enclosed environment, it doesn't have to be. You can plant terrariums in open containers. The tall walls will still retain the humidity around the plants.

You can take any pot and turn it into a terrarium by using a garden cloche (pictured on the right side of the photo of the terrarium containers). Cloches were originally used to protect tender plants from frosts in English gardens. Today they make elegant tops to terrariums.

Look for terrarium containers in housewares and home-goods stores. Cake stands, trifle bowls, and even barware (decanters) can all make great containers.

Repurposing Containers for Miniature Gardens

If a container will hold soil, it can be made into a miniature garden pot. As with containers made specifically for plants, some are better for indoor gardens and some are better for outdoor gardens. Pottery, glass, and ceramic containers hold up longer than wooden or metal containers.

Look in thrift shops and at garage sales for interesting containers to plant. I found this wooden basket (opposite, bottom right) at a consignment shop. It's surprisingly sturdy. It inspired the rustic farm-stand miniature kitchen garden that I planted in it. Because the garden is an indoor garden, I used a deep plastic liner inside the basket.

You can see that there are as many choices for containers as there are accessories for miniature gardens. Whatever you choose, just make sure the container isn't an afterthought. The container's durability, in particular, impacts the long-term growth, and therefore your enjoyment, of your miniature garden.

A large clamshell serves as a container for a miniature succulent garden at Rebecca Sweet's house.

This succulent garden is planted in a wooden cigar box. The quote says, "You might give some serious thought to thanking your lucky stars you're in Texas!"

An old red wagon provides a mobile platform for this miniature garden that showcases accessories at a garden center.

The wood of the basket blends well with the wooden posts of the "Vegetables for Sale" sign used in the garden.

Chapter 4
ACCESSORIES AND THEMES

Teeny tiny accessories are what make mini-gardens mini-gardens. Selecting accessories is one of the most fun parts of creating a miniature garden. There are so many cute, interesting, and tempting little patio sets, pots, birdbaths, animals, and more that it's hard to stop with just a few. (I speak from experience.) Accessories are what make a potful of plants into a tiny garden that you feel you could walk into and sit down in. Accessories establish a theme and tell a story.

Whether you buy accessories or make your own, you're certain to have fun with this part of miniature gardening.

Accessories turn a collection of plants into a tiny universe.

Selecting Miniature Garden Accessories

Miniature gardening (and fairy gardening) is so popular that it's becoming increasingly easier to find furniture, paving materials, and other accessories. When choosing accessories, ask these questions:

- Where will the garden live, indoors or out?
- What is the scale of the accessories in relation to each other and to the plants?
- What is the style or theme of the garden, rustic or formal? Woods or desert? Historic or modern?

Source

You can find miniature garden accessories everywhere. Flea markets are an excellent place to find small figurines or discarded dollhouse furniture. The Etsy website and other handmade marketplaces are filled with artists and crafters selling accessories specifically made for fairy gardens and miniature gardens. You can also find a lot of animals by looking through ceramic offerings on these sites.

Craft stores stock fewer miniatures than they used to, but it's worth a peek in the dollhouse section. You can find materials for making your own accessories throughout the entire craft store—from the cake decorating aisle to the woodworking section, and even the jewelry and bead area.

Model train stores—online and brick-and-mortar—are also good places to shop for accessories.

The Wild Wild West Garden includes handmade accessories purchased from Etsy (the ceramic chameleon and the small cacti) and mass-manufactured accessories from a garden center (skeleton and steer head).

Cupcakes ready for a fairy to eat.

This red bicycle is a popular fairy garden accessory. You'll find it at almost every store that sells miniature garden furniture. Why is it so popular? Probably because it easily helps the viewer connect to the garden. Everyone knows what size a bicycle is in real life. Adding one to the garden creates an instant sense of scale.

Scale

As discussed in the design chapter, it's important to consider scale when selecting miniature garden accessories. If the lounging cat you place on a patio is bigger than the bench it's sitting next to, the mini-garden goes from a little scene to a big mess. Rain boots should be about the same size as chair legs. Miniature food shouldn't be bigger than the plate it's sitting on.

Anyone can picture himself or herself in this scene, sitting at a bistro table, sipping coffee and reading the paper in the morning.

Some dried bits of ornamental grass serve as "straw" in the chicken run, completing the look and finishing the story.

A chicken coop and rustic garden accessories are right for this mini-garden effect. Wrought iron would look out of place in this garden.

A woodland garden needs a campfire. This tiny fire circle, woodpile, and marshmallow sticks were handmade by an artist on Etsy.

Story

The story could also be called the theme of the miniature garden. With so many adorable accessories available, it's hard to choose and stick to a theme. That's why you'll end up with so many mini-gardens eventually—or why you'll end up changing your accessories from time to time. You'll find two patio sets at the garden center (like I did) and require two totally different gardens to put them in.

Can you see yourself sitting in your miniature garden? Do you chuckle when you look at the tableau you've created? Would you like to take a stroll through the botanical garden you planted? If your imagination takes off where the garden ends, you've succeeded in telling a story with your miniature garden.

Have fun with miniature gardening. Not everything has to be serious.

Two patio sets with two very different styles.

Style

Style goes hand in hand with the story or theme. To create a realistic effect, the components of the scene must look like they belong together. Decorating a miniature garden is not unlike decorating a room of your house. Victorian gardens are created with wrought-iron furniture and intricate arbors. A rustic hideaway requires wooden benches and Adirondack chairs and a rough-stone patio. Mushrooms don't really grow in the desert, so they don't belong in a desert garden, but they'd look right at home in a hobbit garden in the woods.

Location

Where will the garden live after it's planted? Plastic accessories hold up the best in outdoor gardens, with metal coming in a close second. Wooden accessories will last for a few seasons. Paper accessories should only be used in indoor gardens or for special-occasion decorating.

The humid environment of an enclosed terrarium is best suited for ceramic, resin, or plastic accessories.

Mini-Garden Mulch

Furniture is just part of the picture in the mini-garden. Mulch adds a finishing touch to the mini-garden just as it does to a regular-sized garden. The mulch layer you use depends on what's in your garden.

Tumbled glass and pottery shards are available for bulk purchase.

Moss is a good mulch for terrariums and woodland gardens. You can purchase sheet moss (left) and preserved reindeer moss (right) or harvest moss from your own garden (top).

Use seashells as mulch in an underwater garden or around succulents.

Polished stones provide an elegant finish to this terrarium planting.

Skip the Sand

Only one garden in this book uses sand as the finishing mulch. When you water a garden with sand covering it, the soil blends with the sand and dribbles and runs. It's messy.

Stuff on a Stick

Shop for mini-garden accessories and you'll find lots of things on sticks. (These are called "picks.") That's to make the items easier to place into the garden. Dollhouses have flat surfaces, so their accessories are less likely to roll around. If you grab a dollhouse miniature for your mini-garden and find that it won't stay in place, use some hot glue to attach a skinny dowel, bamboo skewer, or piece of floral wire to the back or bottom so that you can stick the accessory into the soil where it will stay put.

Three types of mulch: tumbled glass, smooth polished stones, and pea gravel.

Miniature garden accessory picks come in all styles, sizes, and colors.

Steppingstones on top of small gravel make a path from the garden gate to the fairy house.

Pathways and Patios

Put your miniature garden furniture on a patio to make it stand out. Build a garden path to create a sense of movement within the garden. There are many options for miniature garden pathways and patios.

Steppingstones

You can find tiny bricks, little flagstones, and molded mosaic steppingstones to create garden pathways.

This pathway is made from tiles on a mat. All you have to do is cut to size and place in the garden.

Preformed Patios

One option for a patio is to purchase a resin, wood, or stone patio that's preformed for the purpose of showcasing patio furniture.

DIY Patios and Paths

You don't have to buy an already-formed patio for your mini-garden. You can make your own.

Tile Sample Patio

Purchase a piece of tile mat at the hardware store and cut a piece that's large enough to fit whatever you want to sit on it (a fountain, patio set, and so forth). Lay it on the soil and sprinkle sand over it. (You can use patio-setting sand for this.)

Use a foam brush to brush the sand into the cracks between the tiles and to clean off the patio.

Pebble Patios and Paths

You can use regular pea gravel or fairy-sized gravel to make a patio or pathway. If you can find fairy gravel or very fine gravel, use it, as it will look more realistic as a garden path. If you have two sizes or colors of gravel you can use one to make a path (use the smaller-sized gravel for this) and use one as mulch.

To Edge or Not to Edge?

You may want to use a thin metal edge or a wooden edge to contain the gravel from your patio, but you don't have to.

You may also just pour the gravel in the general shape you want for a less formal feel.

Popsicle sticks form an edge for this fairy garden path.

Two sizes of gravel. On the left is "fairy garden gravel," which is very fine. On the right is regular pea gravel, which is the size of, well, a pea.

Making Your Own Mini-Accessories

You can customize mini-garden accessories to make them stand out from the background and add color.

Dollhouse accessories usually require a bit of work before they're fit for the mini-garden. I wanted a "door" for my Backyard Pool garden, so I found one in the dollhouse construction materials. It had a glass window and a hinge, but it needed to be painted. It also had no way to stand up without being affixed to a dollhouse. A few dowels glued to either side of the back of the door and we were in business (see the facing page). (You have to imagine the rest of the house.)

Useful tools for making and customizing accessories include paint, paint brushes, floral picks, corsage pins, floral wire, and pliers. Not pictured: a glue gun and glue sticks—a must.

Painting wrought-iron accessories adds color to the garden. A foam brush makes easy work of this type of project.

(Below) Why get stuck with a specific style of fairy house or potting shed? You can grab an unfinished house or birdhouse and customize it to match your look. Francine, a miniature gardener in my town, took a plain cottage and embellished it with shingles made from pinecones, "siding" made from birch bark, and lichens for detailing.

(Above) This was a vanity table for a dollhouse. I made two small shelves from popsicle sticks, took the drawer out, and painted the whole shelf to create a potting bench.

(Right) The blue door for the mini-garden was inspired by an antique blue farmhouse door I've had in my apartments and houses ever since I've lived on my own.

The completed fairy house is right at home in this woodland garden.

Making a Fairy House

You can make your own fairy house by starting with a plastic cup.

Materials

Plastic cup, paint, twigs, glue gun and glue sticks, and moss.

1. Cut a "door" in one side of the top of the cup.

2. Soften the plastic glare by painting the cup with a contrasting color.

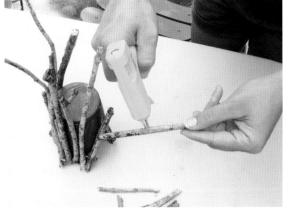

3. Glue the twigs around the fairy house. Vary the length of the twigs for a more rustic effect.

4. Fill in the gaps between sticks by gluing moss to the house.

5. Use moss around the top and bottom of the fairy house to fill in the "chinks" between the twigs.

A simple woven twig fence in one of the children's miniature gardens displayed at the San Francisco Flower and Garden Show.

Twig Pergola

Sticks and twigs are free. You can build almost anything out of them, including fences, pergolas, trellises, and tiny tomato cages. This twig pergola was put to good use in the garden.

Materials

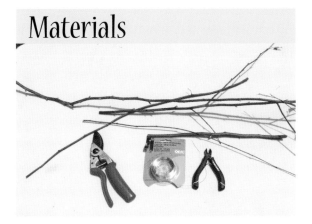

Twigs, pruners, wire cutters, and thin-gauge wire.

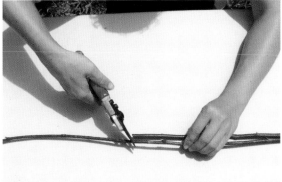

1. Cut the four corner post twigs so that they are about the same length.

2. Cut 8 inches of wire to wire each twig joint together.

3. Place the wire under the first two twigs, crossed.

4. Wrap the wire around one set of opposing crosses and then around the opposite set to stabilize the twigs. Repeat with each joint.

5. Some beaded wire wrapped loosely around the top of the pergola completes the look and adds some "hippie chic." You can also use miniature fairy garden lights for this.

Twinkling lights in the tree next to the door add a realistic touch.

Decorating for the Holidays

Want to have even more fun with your mini-garden? Decorate for the holidays.

Christmas

This is probably the easiest holiday for mini-decorating because there are tons of Christmas miniatures available, including tiny lights.

Snowmen ornaments with their hooks removed serve as table decorations.

This tiny Christmas tree was part of a Christmas ornament. I just used wire clippers to "liberate" it so that it could decorate the bistro table.

Little metal snowflakes
from the Christmas
wrapping aisle and a
chain made from twist ties
decorate this mini-garden.

Christmas Tree Chain

You could make a little chain out of paper, but any stray water would make a
mess of it in short order. Instead, I used multi-colored twist ties from the cake-
decorating area of the craft store.

Materials

Small gauge wire, twist ties, needle nose pliers, and wire cutters.

1. Thread a twist tie through the link below it (or make the first link if you're starting the chain). Form a circle with a twist tie (you can wrap it around your index finger to gauge the size). Leave a short end out to twist.

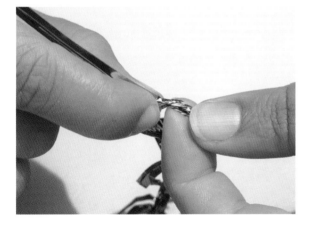

2. Twist the short end around the link. You can wrap the longer end around the loop once before cutting it, as well.

3. Cut off the long end of the tie and wrap the newly cut end around the link so that it lies flat. Repeat. Repeat. Repeat. Periodically test the chain length on the tree, fence, or area where you want to use it. You can use the small-gauge wire on either end of the chain to secure it to the tree.

Halloween

These Halloween decorations are a mixture of purchased accessories and homemade touches.

A ghost roasts marshmallows. The marshmallow stick is hot-glued into the folds of the ghost "sheet."

My husband, Joe, apparently met an untimely end in the Wild Wild West. (I customized the headstone with a black permanent marker.) The grave mounds are made from potting soil. If you want, you can mold little soil mounds by mixing some soil and glue together, forming the mounds, and letting them dry.

A wide view of the Wild Wild West Garden decorated for Halloween.

The pumpkins on the table are made from marbles. I put a dab of hot glue on the bottom to make a flat surface for them to stand up. Several coats of orange paint, and some floral wire twisted and glued to the tops and the pumpkins were ready for prime time.

A hand reaches out from the grave. Is it for you?

July Fourth

The same garden decorated for Christmas looks equally festive for the Fourth of July. Some stickers from the scrapbooking section of a craft store, a miniature American flag on a realistic-looking flagpole, and some confetti do the trick.

You can use twist ties and hot glue to make fireworks. Green floral wire lets the fireworks float in the "sky" above the garden.

No picnic is complete without a cold beverage, or six.

Miniature garden maintenance is quick work.

Chapter 5

GROWING THE MINIATURE GARDEN

Miniature garden maintenance is pretty easy. The gardens are, after all, tiny. That being said, there are some techniques you need to master to care for the living plants and the accessories in the garden.

Excitement over accessories makes it easy to forget that you're maintaining living plants. All plants need:

- Air
- Water
- Light
- Nutrients

If you provide plants with what they need, you're less likely to have problems with pests or diseases.

Care of Living Plants

To keep plants healthy, follow these general guidelines:

- House plants in the conditions they like. Set sun plants in the sun. Plant terrariums with moisture-loving plants. Plant ferns in the shade.
- Rotate indoor plants so that they grow evenly. You can tell it's time to do this when you notice that all of the plants are leaning or growing in one direction. Rotate the container 120 degrees to help the plants straighten out.
- Leave outdoor plants outside except for brief trips indoors to serve as a centerpiece.
- Set indoor plants outside in dappled shade during the summer, if possible.
- Use commercial potting soil (which is sterile) to prevent fungal and bacterial problems around the plant roots.
- Water when the soil is dry, not on a calendar schedule.
- Fertilize occasionally.

All plants grow better outside than they do in the house. The low humidity and cool air inside coupled with lack of natural predators stresses houseplants. You'll be amazed at how a flailing indoor garden will perk up when allowed to grow outside for a few weeks. (Just don't put the indoor garden outside in hot direct sun.)

Mini-Garden Maintenance

You can use some regular full-sized tools for your mini-garden, but you'll find it useful to have some additional items in your tool basket that work like tiny versions of full-sized tools.

Tools
- Watering: A small houseplant watering can (smaller opening), mist bottle, and turkey baster
- Trimming: Scissors and pruners
- Digging: Shovel for scooping soil and a spoon for planting
- Raking: Dinner fork
- Decorating: Long tweezers

Some garden centers have terrarium-specific tools. You can also order them online. The long tweezers with rubber tips are an example of this. They seem frivolous until you need them to place a bit of moss or a shell inside a terrarium with a small opening.

Tools for miniature garden care and maintenance.

Long tweezers make it much easier to place decorative moss in this hurricane vase terrarium.

Scissors are fine for trimming. If you need to remove a branch thicker than a bamboo skewer, you might want to use pruners.

Routine Care Tasks

Calling these "tasks" makes them seem more arduous than they are. They're more like activities. Here are some activities you'll engage in routinely to keep the mini-garden growing.

Trimming

Use scissors to trim groundcovers that are taking over the garden. If the plants are growing over your accessories (and they're not supposed to be), they need a haircut. All of the plants recommended in this book respond well to trimming. Annuals will grow fuller and bushier when they're trimmed.

Cutting off the flowers from an *Ajuga* plant.

Deadheading

Some annuals and perennials you plant will flower. To keep the plants growing and looking tidy, use scissors to cut off the spent flowers.

Watering

Watering is one of the touchiest aspects of plant maintenance. Many people are scared to prune or trim, but plants will usually grow back if you cut too much off while pruning. It is harder to fix problems with watering. Too much water and the plants will rot from the roots up. Not enough water and the plants will wilt or dry up.

There are two ways to decide when to water, and you can use both.

1. **Check the soil.** Stick your finger in the pot or the garden. If the top inch of soil is dry, water. This is the less precise method but works well for more novice gardeners.

2. **Wait until your plants indicate they need water.** Succulents will turn grayish and dull when they need water. They may start to shrivel slightly. Other plants will also become a bit less shiny and will wilt and become limp. If you can learn to recognize when your plants need water before they actually wilt, you'll be able to take better care of them.

Always direct the watering can spout at the base of the plants. Watering the leaves can spread disease.

Watering an outdoor miniature garden.

Use a turkey baster to water plants in a miniature garden.

You can use a turkey baster to water terrariums or individual plants in a miniature garden. A turkey baster allows you to water the plants without worrying about scattering the gravel or mulch in the garden. Basters are also handy for watering plants in small pots within the mini-gardens.

Turkey basters are handy to water plants inside small pots inside the miniature garden.

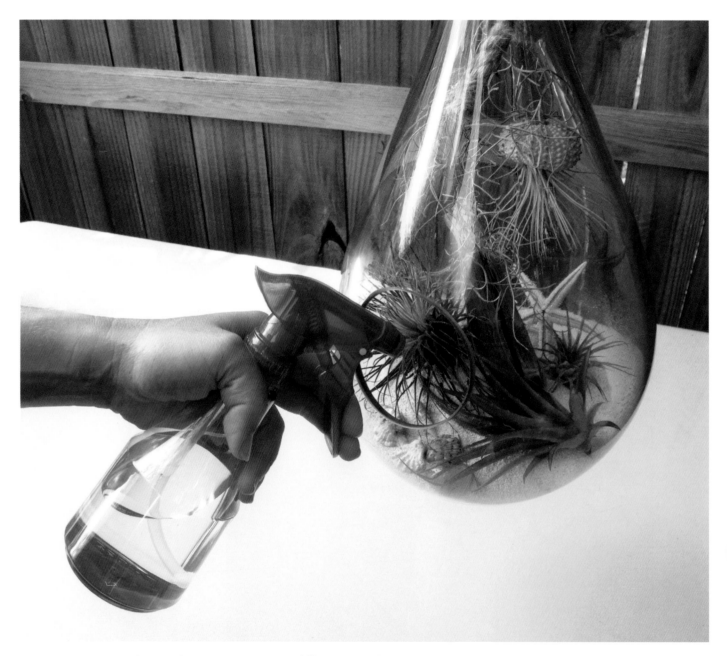

Misting air plants in a hanging terrarium. It would be impractical to remove the plants in order to water them. Air plants need to be dunked in water or misted to stay hydrated. Mist air plants until they're dripping wet twice a week or dunk in water once a week.

Cleaning the mini-patio with the spray bottle.

Keeping Plants Clean

Are the plants dusty or dirty? Do you need to clean off the patio? The same spray bottle that you use to water air plants can be used to "hose down" the garden.

Pest Control

Most miniature gardens won't have pest issues unless they're severely stressed. If you see insects on the leaves (usually indicated by white "fluff" on the leaves) you can wipe the leaves off with a moist paper towel.

Flying black insects are fungus gnats that cause problems if the soil is too wet. Simply cut back on watering and they'll go away.

Plants in outdoor gardens are more likely to be chewed on than indoor plants. Handpick insects when you can. Use horticultural oil (for hard-bodied insects such as beetles) or insecticidal soap (for soft-bodied insects such as aphids) when you have large infestations. Alternatively, you could just dig up the affected plant and replace it.

Fertilizing

Mini-gardens need little food in order to thrive. If you're keeping a garden in the same pot for several years, it is worth feeding with a diluted liquid fertilizer a few times a year. Follow the instructions for mixing on the fertilizer label, but mix it at half strength. Water the plants as you normally would, only with the fertilizer. You can feed quarterly. Make a note on the calendar so that you'll remember to feed.

Part 2
CREATING MINIATURE AND FAIRY GARDEN PROJECTS

You have the basics under your belt, so now you are ready to plant some mini-gardens. There are fourteen projects in this section to help you get started. You can recreate them exactly as you see them demonstrated here, or you can use them for inspiration and design your own.

Part 1 gave you pointers and guidelines so that you can achieve a realistic miniature garden look with plants and accessories to scale, but don't feel you have to limit yourself to those directions or these project outlines. Let your imagination take over.

The one rule you really should follow is to put plants together that need similar growing conditions. If you skip that, you won't be successful because your plants won't grow.

Along that line, Part 2 is organized by the "end use" of the garden:

- Indoor Miniature and Fairy Gardens
- Terrariums and Aeriums
- Outdoor Miniature and Fairy Gardens

Each project description includes suggestions for appropriate plants and accessories for each type of garden. I hope seeing these projects will give you ideas for your own garden themes.

This garden reminds me of my time spent managing historic botanical gardens.

Chapter 6
INDOOR MINIATURE AND FAIRY GARDENS

What makes an indoor garden different from an outdoor miniature garden? The plant selection. Houseplants, air plants, and some succulents grow well indoors. Most perennials and annual flowers just don't do as well inside.

Advantages of indoor miniature gardens:
- You have greater flexibility with accessories (you don't have to worry about weather).
- You aren't constrained by hardiness zones in plant selection.

Challenges of indoor miniature gardens:
- You have to use plants that need lower amounts of light.
- You must be careful not to overwater.

All indoor miniature gardens will benefit from getting the chance to grow outside during the summer. Set the garden under a tree or on a screened porch where it will get bright, indirect light. Natural predators will attack any pests that might be on the plants. More humid air and brighter sunlight will cause the plants to perk up. Just make sure to remove any paper, cardboard, or wooden accessories (that you don't want to weather) until you move them back inside.

An indoor garden serves as a centerpiece and conversation starter.

Bring some of the West to your desk with an indoor garden.

Wild Wild West

I've always loved visiting the desert, but the idea of moving so far away from the ocean isn't for me. To give myself a bit of the West on the East Coast, I planted a Wild Wild West Garden. If you live somewhere with slow-draining soil that's inhospitable to succulents or want to grow some "sunshine" to get you through a long winter, plant a western-themed indoor garden. This garden was inspired by the turquoise blue patio furniture, which reminded me of the painted metal chairs my grandparents had on their farm when I was little. If only we'd kept those!

Materials

The blue in the chameleon repeats the blue of the patio furniture and ties the design together.

Succulents are a must for a western-themed garden.

Accessories
Turquoise patio set
Twig pergola (See instructions for making this in Chapter 4)
Ceramic chameleon
Ceramic horned toad
Skeleton
Ceramic cacti
Rusty metal fence
Steer head skeleton

Plants
Plants in the Wild Wild West Garden don't fit neatly into categories of "trees," "shrubs," and groundcovers. There are taller plants and shorter plants to create layers of interest. All of the plants in this garden are succulents or cacti. There are a few air plants artfully placed to look like tumbling tumbleweeds.

Tall Plants
Aloe spp., aloe
Crassula spp., jade plant

Short Plants
Sempervivum spp., hens and chickens (or hens and chicks)
Sedum spp.
Cacti (there are many genera and types of cacti)

Sizing Animals
When looking for animals to "live" in your garden, try to find some that are smaller than the furniture. In terms of scale, the horned toad and chameleon used in this garden would be awfully big if I met them for real out in the wild.

Because this is an indoor garden, the specific genus of the succulents doesn't really matter. You don't have to check for cold-hardiness. As long as all of the plants will thrive with the same general light requirement, you'll be OK with whatever you choose.

Container
This garden is planted in a rectangular, plastic self-watering container. It is 22 inches by 18 inches by 6 inches deep. The self-watering part isn't important for this garden, but it's fairly easy to find large, square shallow containers when you look at the self-watering section. People use them to grow patio vegetables.

I kept the drain holes plugged in this container, so I'll have to avoid overwatering.

Potting Soil

Mix perlite with potting soil to create a lightweight cacti and succulent mix.

Wild Wild West
Step by Step

1. Fill the container with the amended potting soil mixture. Place the largest accessory—in this case, the pergola—first. It will provide a framework for the other elements and plants.

2. Position the plants in the garden to check spacing before planting. That way, if you have extra plants, you won't have disturbed their roots by taking them out of their pots. (You can plant a different garden with any extras.)

3. Plant the plants. You can take the pergola out if you leave the plants in their pots in place. I used the sedum as "shrubs" behind and around the pergola.

4. Add the mulch. Light-colored pea gravel keeps with the western color palette without being as messy as sand.

Tip: I used some broken tumbled pottery and glass in a different color in order to create a kind of "dry river" through the garden. You can see that in front of the patio set.

5. Place the accessories. The cacti are specimen plants in this garden and are planted around the front right corner of the pergola. A horned toad keeps watch next to them. Water the garden to settle the plants. You want the soil to be damp but not soaking wet.

A hand-painted chameleon enjoys "shade" from the aloe plant.

Care and Maintenance

The biggest challenge with this garden is watering correctly. If in doubt, let the plants and soil dry out a bit between watering. You shouldn't have to water these plants more than once a week if the garden is outside and every two weeks if it's inside. Keep an eye on the plants; if they look gray or shriveled, they need water.

To water the air plants (one is along the edge of the front of the garden and two are along the right side of the garden) just pick them up and soak them in a bowl of water for an hour once a week.

This garden looks great when decorated for Halloween. It turns into a combination of an abandoned gold-mining ghost town and a haunted house.

Backyard Poolscape

It's fun to make a miniature garden that looks like a backyard so that you can decorate it for holidays. You might recognize this indoor miniature garden from the Christmas and Fourth of July photos in Chapter 4. This is a large garden, and therefore can hold more accessories, offering plenty of space to personalize it. One finishing touch that doesn't necessarily photograph well, but that is fun when you see the garden in person, is the addition of little resin songbirds perching in the trees and on furniture. My friend whose hands are featured in many of these photographs is an environmental scientist who works with birds. When I see the birds in this garden, I think of her.

Materials

The picnic table and bistro set were painted to customize them and add color to the garden.

Accessories

Dollhouse door, painted
Bistro table and chairs, painted
Picnic table, painted
Preformed miniature garden pool
Square of bathroom tile mat
Resin garden gnome
Ceramic birdbath
Ceramic dogs
Resin songbirds
Metal lantern and shepherd's hook
Resin turtle
Folded newspaper
Coffee cup and saucer
Terra cotta pots
Metal trellis
Sun hat
Soda bottles in caddy

Plants
"Trees"
Ficus benjamina, ficus tree
Cupressus macrocarpa 'Wilma Goldcrest', Wilma Goldcrest (Monterey) cypress

"Shrubs"
Table ferns
Ophiopogon japonicus 'Nanus', dwarf mondo grass
Hypoestes phyllostachya, polka dot plant
Saxifraga stolonifera, strawberry begonia

"Groundcovers"
Ficus pumila var. *quercifolia*, oak leaf creeping fig
Pilea glauca 'Aquamarine', friendship plant

Container
The container is a plastic planting dish that's 20 inches across by 8 inches deep. Because it is an indoor garden, the drainage holes remain plugged.

Potting Soil
This garden uses regular bagged potting soil (*not* topsoil).

Backyard Poolscape Step by Step

1. Fill the container with potting soil. Leave about 2 inches between the top of the container and the top of the soil. Lay the patio. Set the tile patio square on the soil where you'd like it in the container. Then top it with sand and use a foam brush to sweep sand into the cracks between the tiles. This is the "mortar" in the patio.

2. Place the door. The door is the anchoring accessory and a focal point in the garden. Everything else—plants and accessories—will be added to the garden in relation to the door and to the patio onto which it opens.

3. Position the plants. When you plant a garden this large, with so many plants and accessories, you'll have to play around with placement. If you're using a pool, you can set it on top of the soil to save the space while you position and plant the other plants. Save "digging in" the pool for last so that it doesn't fill up with soil.

Mondo Grass: Indoor or Outdoor Plant?
Dwarf mondo grass is an outdoor plant, but you can "cheat" and keep it inside for several months. Because its texture is unique among miniature garden plants, it's worth planting and then spending a few dollars to replace it every now and then.

4. Plant the plants. Varying sizes and textures keep the plants from blending in to one another. There's a reason why dwarf mondo grass is in almost every miniature garden—the grassy form is unlike almost any other plant suited to miniature gardening—most grasslike plants just aren't small enough.

5. Place the pool. Wait until all plants are planted to place the pool and fill it. Otherwise, it will get soil and rocks in it. You can clean the pool by removing it and washing it in the sink. You can also suck out the water with a turkey baster, wipe the pool out with a towel, and then refill it.

6. Introduce accessories. The picnic table in this garden has been painted to add some color. Instead of setting it on a patio (tile or gravel), it is sitting on two creeping fig groundcover plants. I'm not a big fan of placing accessories right on bare soil, but neither do I want every single garden to be covered in gravel or mulch. Truly flat-growing groundcovers such as the oak-leafed fig bridges the gap.

7. Add pathways. Build your miniature garden like you'd build a full-sized garden. If you'd put a pathway between a patio and another seating area in your full-sized garden, put one in your miniature garden too. Pathways can add a sense of flow in a miniature garden. Your eye naturally moves from one seating area to the next, over the pathway. Water the garden until the soil is as damp as a wrung-out sponge.

Adding Finishing Touches

Take your miniature garden to the next level by adding accessories such as dishes, books, miniature coolers, and food. The newspaper and coffee cup sitting on the bistro table give the impression that someone just stepped away from the garden and will be right back. Larger gardens offer more space to include these types of accessories without overwhelming the plants.

A handmade ceramic birdbath next to the patio adds an artistic touch.

Plant small ferns in miniature urns to sit on the patio. Use an eyedropper or turkey baster to water these mini-gardens within the mini-garden.

Even miniature gardens need lighting. Instead of randomly placing a lantern, think about where someone sitting in the garden would most benefit from its light.

Care and Maintenance

The ficus tree next to the blue door is the most temperamental plant in this garden. Sudden changes in environment (such as moving the plant from outside to inside or vice versa) can cause it to drop its leaves. Just keep an eye on it. If it loses its leaves, it isn't necessarily dead. Give it a few weeks to grow new ones before you replace the plant.

Dwarf mondo grass is an outdoor plant and, as such, will need to be replaced from time to time. If it turns brown, it's time to replant.

All of the plants can be trimmed with scissors to maintain their size and shape.

This kitchen garden can sit on the kitchen counter or in the kitchen window, providing fresh herbs and microgreens, year-round.

Mini-Kitchen Garden

Many mini-gardens require little to no care, other than adding or changing accessories, once they've been planted. If you want to actually "tend" a little garden, this is the project for you. The Mini-Kitchen Garden uses herbs such as parsley and sage for the "trees" and polka dot plants (non-edible) for shrubs. Inside the tiny picket fence, there's a pot-within-a-pot where you can plant seeds for microgreens. (You can *buy* microgreens at the store or at a farmers market, but they're expensive.) My favorite accessory in this garden is the clothesline that holds the "Vegetables for Sale" sign. It was handmade by an Etsy artist, but was too large, in scale, for the other projects in this book. It blends perfectly with the rustic container for this garden.

Materials

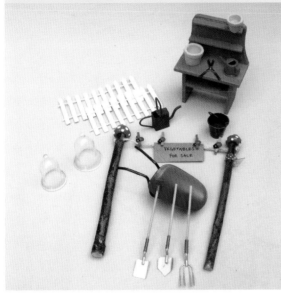

Plant your miniature kitchen garden with herbs.

Red is a unifying color throughout these accessories. Remember, you can repeat a color in accessories as well as plants to achieve repetition in the garden.

Accessories
White picket fence
Miniature garden cloches
Handmade ladybug clothesline
Watering cans
Tiny loppers (hedge trimmers)
Terra cotta pots
Bucket
Wheelbarrow
Long-handled garden tools
Potting bench

Beets, turnips, mustard, and beans are all easy to grow as microgreens.

Plants
Select herbs to use as trees and shrubs in this miniature garden. Instead of the polka dot plant (used for shrubs in front of the fence), you could also plant thyme. I didn't plant the chives because the container was too small, but they work well as indoor herbs and have a nice "grassy" look.

Container
This container is a wooden basket made from branches coiled and nailed together. It has a slice of wood for the base. It's quite sturdy; even when planted, you can still carry the garden around by the handle. You could plant a kitchen garden like this in any basket, as long as you put a plastic liner in it to hold the soil. A handle makes the garden easy to move around.

Place a plastic liner inside a "found object" container if the container is not watertight or has gaps where soil could escape.

Potting Soil
Use sterilized soilless seedling mix for this miniature garden to ensure quick germination of the microgreen seeds while avoiding fungal problems.

Mini-Kitchen Garden Step by Step

1. Place the liner in the basket and fill with potting soil up to 2 inches from the top. Poke holes in the bottom of a plastic container and fill it with soil. Sink it into the soil in the larger container so that the lip is just below the soil surface. The purpose of the "pot within a pot" is to make it easier to dig out and replace the soil where the microgreens are growing from time to time without disrupting all of the other plants.

2. Plant the larger plants around the plastic container that you buried in step 2.

3. Place the fence around the container so that you know where to "dig" to plant microgreen seeds. Use the tiny shovel (or the end of a pencil) to dig ¼-inch furrows in the microgreen garden.

4. Sow the microgreens thickly in the garden and cover with ¼ inch of the sterilized seedling mix. Water until the soil is about as damp as a wrung-out sponge. Keep the seeds moist as they are sprouting. You can use the spray bottle to mist them. That should provide enough water to keep them damp.

5. Place the accessories and wait for the microgreens to grow.

6. Use kitchen scissors to snip the microgreens off at the soil line when they have their first set of true leaves (which will look like the second set of leaves). You can resow in the same soil up to five or six times. (You only get one harvest from each sowing.)

Using Microgreens
Use microgreens as a garnish for any formal dinner occasion. Add them to salads for an extra nutrient boost. (You can harvest enough microgreens from this miniature garden to provide about ¼ cup once a week.)

Care and Maintenance
Change the soil in the microgreen garden after five or six harvests. Use a spoon to scoop out the soil. You might find it helpful to premoisten the new soil before you place it in the miniature garden.

The weathered wooden "fence" container provides a finished look for this beach-themed garden.

Garden at the Beach

Even if you live nowhere near the beach, you can still plant your own little paradise. This garden is a vacation in a pot. You can't help but relax when you look at it. Small succulents stand in for their larger counterparts that natively grow along beaches. Tumbled glass mulch forms the water, while aquarium sand covers the beach. The featured plant in this garden is a screw pine seedling (they grow to be 15-foot-tall trees along the beaches in Florida), but you could also use a jade plant, aloe, or other large treelike succulent as a focal point.

Materials

Notice that the bucket of shells is perfectly sized to sit on the beach chair.

Place a liner inside the container.

Accessories

Driftwood
Tumbled glass mulch
Seashells from the beach
Beach chair
Beach bucket filled with shells
Optional-beach umbrella (not pictured)

If you've gone on a beach vacation and brought back shells or sea glass that you didn't know where to put, your problem is solved. Now you can create a garden to showcase your beachcombing treasures. In a miniature garden larger shells look more like creatures from the deep than diminutive mollusks. To fill a beach bucket in scale with other beach furniture you need to look for teeny *tiny* shells no longer than your pinky fingernail.

Plants

All of the plants used in this garden, with the exception of the screw pine (*Pandanus* spp.) are succulents. The finished garden was planted with hens and chickens (*Sempervivum* spp.) next to the beach chair. *Haworthia* spp. plants on the right side of the screw pine look like the big agaves you often see growing along beaches and dunes. Assorted 1-inch succulents with blue-toned leaves are planted in the "water" section of the garden.

When selecting a "specimen" tree, look for plants that can tolerate the same dry conditions as the succulents.

Container

The metal container did not have drainage holes, so I poked holes in a clear liner and used it inside the metal pan. This container is 12 inches in diameter, but the same style is available in larger and smaller sizes.

Potting Soil

Add perlite to potting soil to create a lightweight mix suitable for succulents.

A tall and grasslike screw pine is the star plant of this grouping.

Garden at the Beach Step by Step

1. Start by poking holes in the liner container. This will allow some drainage in this indoor garden without water dripping through onto your dining room table.

2. Mix the soil by adding one part perlite to two parts potting soil.

3. Place the liner in the container and fill the container with the perlite-amended potting mix.

4. Place the largest plant, the screw pine, in the pot.

5. Arrange the other plants around the screw pine (or other specimen plant) to check spacing before removing them from their pots. Once you're satisfied with spacing, go ahead and plant them.

6. Add the tumbled glass "mulch" for the water. I used larger pieces to outline and smaller pieces between the plants.

7. Use a soup spoon to fill in the "beach" with aquarium sand from the pet store. Aquarium sand is coarser in texture than playground sand and is intended to be around plants and water.

8. Place the furniture and accessories.

Care and Maintenance

As with the other succulent gardens in this book, watering is the chief concern. You don't want to overwater the plants. Use a turkey baster for watering so that you don't scatter sand all over the place. You can set this garden outside during the summer, but bring it in if a heavy rain is forecast. Because there aren't large drainage holes, the garden can get swamped with just 1 inch of rain.

Keep an Eye on the Details

Even within a relatively small garden, there is still room for little vignettes. On one side of the screw pine there's a beach chair and shell bucket. Little sand toys would be cute additions to this area.

I looked all over for a small umbrella that wasn't a paper cocktail umbrella, but couldn't find one. Are you crafty? You might enjoy making your own.

Don't you just want to spend a relaxing afternoon in this little beach chair?

Different haworthia plants represent the large century plants (*Agave* spp.) seen growing along the dunes in coastal areas.

Chapter 7
TERRARIUMS AND AERIUMS

Terrariums have their roots in Wardian cases, small greenhouses the size of a steamer trunk developed by Dr. Nathaniel Ward in 1829 to bring back plant specimens from botanical expeditions. Plants in the Wardian cases could live for months without the addition of water (which was ideal on voyages across the sea during which fresh water was limited). Terrariums today are less bulky and more artistic than the original roughly constructed cases. They can be as large as a side table or as small as a juice glass.

While you might think of a terrarium as a purely enclosed system, you can plant terrariums that are open at one end or another. The tall walls will still elevate the humidity around the plants.

Aeriums are similar to terrariums, but they house plants that don't need soil—air plants. When air plants are enclosed by glass they require less frequent watering and tend to grow better in the dry home environment. (They're native to warm, humid climates.)

Some of the terrariums in this chapter are themed and include accessories, while others are just plants. They're all captivating little worlds.

A hurricane terrarium planted with a parlor palm and other low-light plants is a perfect coffee table or end table decoration.

Choose ceramic or plastic accessories for humid enclosed terrariums.

Where the Dinosaurs Roam

A terrarium filled with tropical plants is the perfect jungle setting in which to keep a dinosaur or two. While you can't time travel back to the age of the dinosaurs, you can bring a little bit of the Jurassic era to your desk or dining room table. Moisture-loving houseplants grow best in this fully enclosed terrarium.

Materials

Accessories

Preserved reindeer moss
Polished stones
Ceramic animal figurines
Handmade ceramic sculptures
Plastic or resin mushrooms
Plastic decorative swirl picks

A container that looks large when not filled with plants and soil suddenly has little room for accessories when planted. Look for accessories, including animal figurines that are less than 2 inches long for larger terrariums and ½ to 1 inch long for smaller terrariums.

Container

This container is a clear candy jar from the craft store. It is 8 inches tall and 7 inches in diameter.

Terrarium plants are usually stocked in the houseplant section of the garden center.

Plants

Ideal terrarium plants like high humidity and low light. Table ferns, polka dot plants, *Selaginella, Croton, Alternanthera*, and *Ficus* plants all fare well in terrariums. Because terrariums are so small, look for plants in 1-inch pots or plants in larger pots that can be split into smaller pieces.

Potting Soil

Use a sterilized seedling mix or potting soil in a terrarium to prevent fungal problems. A small bag from the houseplant section of the garden center is enough for this project. It uses a few cups of soil, at most.

Key ingredients for terrarium construction include sterilized potting soil, activated filter carbon (activated charcoal), and tumbled stones.

Where the Dinosaurs Roam Terrarium Step by Step

1. Fill the bottom of the container with ½ to 1 inch of rocks.

2. Pour activated charcoal on top of the rocks until the rocks are barely covered by the charcoal.

3. Add the potting mix on top of the charcoal. Start with 1 inch of potting mix. This doesn't seem like much, but it is easier to start with a little, then place the plants and fill in around the plants, than it is to add more potting mix and dig holes.

4. Place the plants. If you're using accessories, such as the dinosaur, you can set them in among the plants to gauge the effect see if you want to move the plants around prior to planting.

5. Remove plants from pots and plant them. The bottom of the plant rootballs can be touching the rocks. Use a spoon to fill in with soil around the plants.

6. Add decorative mulches such as preserved reindeer moss or tumbled stones.

7. Position the accessories.

8. Water the terrarium. This is the trickiest step. It's *easy* to overwater and then difficult to get the terrarium to dry out. Start by watering so that the top inch of soil (which might, in this case, be all of the soil) is about as damp as a wrung-out sponge. You can always add water.

9. Place the cover on the terrarium, set it in bright indirect light, and enjoy.

View the Garden from All Sides

Even in such a small terrarium, you can make separate little scenes. Ideally, you'll use accessories to make the terrarium interesting and inviting from all sides.

A friend gave me these mushroom picks for my birthday the year I went through my terrarium-making frenzy. They are a nice detail addition on the other side of the terrarium from the dinosaur.

To the right of the dinosaur is a handmade ceramic sculpture (about 1 inch tall) from Etsy. It came in a set with a birdbath used in the Backyard Poolscape Garden. Just because accessories come in a set together doesn't mean they have to be used together.

Care and Maintenance

Enclosed terrariums have to get some light so that the plants can photosynthesize, grow, and keep the water cycle going. Otherwise the plants will rot. You'll know if the terrarium is getting enough light when you can see some water droplets (condensation) on the inside of the glass.

If the plants start to rot or become mushy, the terrarium is too wet. Open the cover and let it dry out for a week or so. It could take a while to find the right balance of water for the system to reach equilibrium. I have one terrarium that I haven't watered for two years. It can be done.

This recycled-glass hanging terrarium can be planted with anything, but it makes a good showcase for large specimen air plants.

Underwater Aerium

Air plants are beautiful specimens, best viewed from eye-level and close-up. Planting air plants (though you don't really plant—you "place") in a hanging terrarium is a fun way to create a garden with these unusual plants.

The container used for this project is a Roost™ recycled glass terrarium, but you can find other blown glass hanging terrariums. Alternatively, you could create the same type of project in a tall hurricane-style vase.

In addition to the Garden at the Beach, this is another good project with which you can display your vacation beachcombing finds.

Materials

Seashells are a must for this underwater aerium, but please *never* harvest live shells. When beachcombing, determine whether there is a creature inside the shell or if it is empty. If there's a mollusk living inside of it, throw the shell back in the water.

Accessories

Sea urchin shell
Driftwood
Tumbled glass mulch
Sand dollar
Spanish moss
Polished stones
Sea glass
Rope

Tillandsia usneoides, or Spanish moss, grows in the trees of humid southern locations. One long strand is actually many separate living plants. You can collect your own to use in projects, but if it's going to be used inside your house, you should clean it first by boiling it or microwaving it to kill insects that live in the plants.

Container

Air plants can be large. A big container allows you to showcase several of them and make a little underwater scene. This is a Roost recycled glass hanging terrarium (used here as an aerium), but any hanging terrarium would work.

This container can hang from the ceiling or sit on an end table.

Air plants come in a variety of sizes, shapes, and colors.

Plants

Use a variety of air plants (*Tillandsia* spp.) to create this garden. It's becoming easier to find these plants at garden centers, but you can also order them online. If you want a variety of colors and sizes, order single plants. If you order a "package deal," unless the different types are specified in the product description, you could end up with all of the same type.

Tools

A pair of long terrarium tweezers (with rubber grips on the end) and a spray bottle come in handy for assembling and watering the aerium.

Potting Soil

This garden doesn't require potting soil. I used aquarium sand to create the "ocean floor" above which the "creatures" (air plants) will float. You wouldn't have to use sand, but I think it "grounds" the garden and makes it look more like a scene and less like a collection of plants hanging around.

You can find aquarium sand at a pet store.

Mini Project: Floating Jellyfish

Use a sea urchin shell, an air plant, and a piece of fine-gauge wire or fishing line to create a jellyfish to float in your aerium.

A jellyfish swims through the aerium.

1. Bend the wire so that it forms a T and check the air plant for size in the bottom sea urchin opening by sticking the air plant in the bottom of the sea urchin. If the plant is too large, you'll need to *carefully* chip away at the bottom so that you can fit the air plant in it.

2. From the inside of the shell, thread the two ends of the wire through the top hole and pull it so that the T is just inside the top of the shell.

3. Hot glue the air plant inside the sea urchin. Now you have a jellyfish.

Underwater Aerium Step by Step

4. Pour enough aquarium sand into the vessel so that there is 1 inch in the bottom of the aerium. Place the driftwood. If you make a jellyfish, this is the time to hang it by wrapping the wire around the rope.

5. If you're not using a jellyfish, you can anchor an air plant, upside-down, by wedging it between the rope knot and the top of the aerium. If you're using a different type of hanging aerium, you could wire, or even glue, an air plant upside-down.

6. Place the other air plants and accessories. You don't have to "plant" air plants in the sand. You can just sit them artfully around the aerium. The long-handled tweezers come in handy for this part, as it is difficult to get your hand all the way inside the aerium, particularly as you add more plants.

Care and Maintenance

Air plants do need to be watered in order to live. Because it is impractical to take them out of the aerium once it is assembled, use a spray bottle to mist the plants until they're dripping twice a week.

Air plants do bloom, though not on any particular schedule. Once the plant blooms, it will die and a "pup" will form and grow from the bottom side of the plant. Once the parent plant is dead, clip it off and water the baby plant.

Keep a mister handy to water the air plants.

Set the air plants so that their most colorful side is facing out.

Overall, this project isn't complicated. It just takes patience to place all of the plants where you want them, especially in a hanging container that swings while you're working on it. (You can set the container in a bucket or enlist help from a friend to hold it while you decorate.)

Details

You can find sea urchins and clean them, or buy them for the mini-project. Always look for sustainably harvested sea urchins. (They've been picked up from the beach after they're dead and then cleaned, not harvested while they're alive.)

Look around your yard for twigs that have lichen growing on them. Lichen looks a little bit like seaweed. If you don't have driftwood, a lichen-covered twig will add some height and structure.

You can hot glue air plants to twigs or suspend them from wires or fishing line.

This elegant terrarium would make an excellent centerpiece for a dining room table.

Elegant Cloche

Quick to make, this terrarium provides long-lasting, elegant décor for your house. Because it's planted in a terra cotta pot, you'll need to grab a cork trivet with a plastic bottom to put under the pot to protect your furniture. It's easier than ever to find the type of glass cloche that forms the top of the terrarium. Though this container came as a top and bottom set, you can browse through home-goods stores and garden centers and find two pieces that fit together. (Hint: Check the aisle with glassware for appetizers and hors d'oeuvres. Sometimes you'll find cloches that go over a cheese tray.) You can also mix and match the plants inside the container—no need to stick to the exact plant list here. This project would look equally beautiful with an assortment of ferns under glass.

Note: Even though this project is quick in terms of assembly, it's still messy, and unless it's really cold outside, you will probably want to complete it in your garage or backyard instead of at the kitchen table.

Materials

Clockwise from top left: polished stones, activated filter carbon, preserved reindeer moss, rinsed pea gravel.

Accessories

Because you can't see what's in the bottom of this container, I used pea gravel instead of polished stones. Bagged pea gravel can be dusty, so I rinse it before using it so it isn't messy. Find polished black stones and preserved reindeer moss at the craft store or in the houseplant section at the garden center. Activated filter carbon or activated charcoal is in the aquarium section of the pet store. You don't need a large container of it unless you plan to make a lot of terrariums.

Container

The container for this project is a Campo De' Fiori aged terraria with a terra cotta base and hand-blown glass cloche. You can create the same look without the branded container, just test the cloche to make sure it fits the pot. (It should sit just inside or right on the edge of the pot.)

Potting Soil

Use sterilized potting soil for this terrarium project.

Plants

"Tree"
Eugenia myrtifolia 'Nanum', Teenie Genie miniature brush cherry

"Shrub"
Hypoestes phyllostachya, green-and-white polka dot plant

"Groundcover"
Ficus pumila var. *quercifolia,* creeping fig

The glass cloche is perfectly sized to fit over the terra cotta container.

Elegant Cloche
Step by Step

1. Cover the bottom of the container with pea gravel to a depth of ½ inch.

2. Top the pea gravel with activated filter carbon. This layer should only be ⅛ inch thick.

3. Add potting soil, leaving 1 inch between the top of the soil and the top of the container.

4. Plant the plants, starting with the largest plant first. Fill in with soil around the plants, leaving at least a ¼ to ½ inch of space between the top of the soil and the top of the container.

Care and Maintenance

This terrarium requires more frequent watering than a fully enclosed terrarium in a glass or glass-and-plastic container. That's because the terra cotta pot is porous and water will evaporate from it. You will still need to water it less than a normal potted houseplant. Check the soil every couple of weeks by sticking your finger in it. The soil should remain evenly moist. If it is dry, water the terrarium.

5. Add decorative moss around the plants, if you want to dress it up a bit.

6. Water the plants. Water this terrarium as you'd water a normal houseplant—until the top inch of soil is damp like a wrung-out sponge. The terra cotta pot will permit more evaporation than an enclosed glass container, so you don't have to be as worried about overwatering.

7. Mulch with decorative stones.

8. Place the glass cloche on top of the container. Set the container in an area of the house with bright, indirect light.

Why put a candle in this hurricane vase when you can grow a beautiful garden?

Hurricane Terrarium

Once an unused wedding gift, a few plants and some decorative moss turned this hurricane vase into an eye-catching garden. You can find large vases like this at every home décor store. The key to its finished look is layering. You can see everything—from the pebbles in the bottom to the palm tree growing out of the top. Speaking of the top, this terrarium isn't enclosed, which gives you greater freedom to use taller plant material.

Materials

Activated filter carbon
Rinsed pea gravel
Hurricane vase
Preserved reindeer moss
Parlor palm
Peperomia plant (not pictured)
Podophyllum, arrowhead plant (not pictured)

This project calls for light-colored pea gravel for the bottom of the container, even though you can see it. That will create a more interesting layered look, whereas using dark colored stones would make the bottom of the container appear "heavy," with the soil and stones creating a dark mass in the bottom.

Potting Soil

Use houseplant potting soil for this project.

Hurricane Terrarium
Step by Step

1. Layer 1 to 1½ inches of gravel in the bottom of the vase.

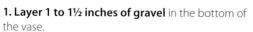
3. Add 2 inches of potting soil to the container.

2. Pour in activated filter carbon to a depth of ½ inch.

4. Place the plants. I split off a smaller chunk of the parlor palm so that it was lighter and more airy in feel. Just plunking the whole palm in the vase looked messy and top-heavy because the palm wasn't tall enough so that the entire top floated above the vase. Once in place, the bottom of the palm looked naked. There was a lot of space between the stems and the leaves, but, again, not enough space so that all of the leaves were above the vase rim.

Adding two shorter plants of contrasting colors and textures around the base of the palm filled in the vase space and created more interest. This is the same layering technique used in full-sized garden design, only the layers of a full-sized garden are trees (tallest), shrubs and large perennials (middle layer), and annual flowers, groundcovers, small perennials, and bulbs (shortest layer).

Use a long-handled spoon to add soil around the plants so that their roots are entirely covered.

5. Add decorative moss around the plants using the terrarium tweezers. Once all of the plants are planted, it's hard to reach all the way into the bottom of the vase. Water the container until you can just see water trickling in between the pebbles at the bottom of the vase.

During the "Great Terrarium Frenzy," I planted this vase with a different type of palm tree. The plant was about 4 inches taller than the container, so when planted, stuck out of the top of the container at least 8 inches, creating a dramatic effect.

Care and Maintenance
This terrarium will dry out faster than a fully enclosed terrarium but more slowly than a regular houseplant. You can see, through the glass, when the soil has started to dry out. It will be lighter in color. That's when it's time to water.

Quick Canning Jar Terrarium

Ideal for a desktop or a child's nightstand, this canning jar terrarium is easy to make and to care for. It's a great school project.

Materials
Rinsed pea gravel
Activated filter carbon
Sterile potting soil
Selaginella plant
Plastic wrap
Wide-mouth canning jar and lid
Animal figurine

Quick Canning Jar Terrarium Step-by-Step
1. Layer pea gravel in the bottom, activated filter carbon on top, and 1 inch of potting soil over that.

2. Use the terrarium tweezers (or a dinner fork) to plant the *Selaginella*. Make sure its roots are in the soil.

3. Water the terrarium until you can see water running into the pebbles.

4. Place the animal figurine next to the side of the jar.

5. Tear off a sheet of plastic wrap and cover the jar with it.

6. Place the lid ring on the jar and screw it down.

7. Use sharp scissors to cut the plastic wrap so that the edges aren't visible under the lid.

(Using plastic wrap instead of its metal lid allows more light to reach the plant and a better view of the plant.)

Look for hardy succulents to grow well in outdoor miniature gardens.

Chapter 8
OUTDOOR MINIATURE AND FAIRY GARDENS

Outdoor miniature gardens are excellent conversation pieces when placed near the front door or on a patio or screened-in porch. These gardens are planted with plants hardy to the growing zone where the gardener lives.

While you can plant outdoor miniature and fairy gardens that use accessories and props, you can also plant miniature gardens that showcase just plants that you can't easily grow in the ground where you live or that would disappear in a full-sized garden.

If you have the space, you can plant a miniature in-ground garden. These are especially useful if you have larger "mini" plants such as a dwarf conifer or miniature hosta collection. You can also use larger accessories in in-ground gardens.

If you're growing a plant in a container above ground, subtract one hardiness zone from what the plant tag says. For example, a plant that's hardy to zone 5 will likely only be hardy to zone 6 if it's grown in a container.

I created this for my grandma who now lives in an apartment with a porch. This miniature garden is filled with personal touches that remind me of the full-sized gardens she had while I was growing up.

Grandma's Garden

While visiting my mom the summer I worked on this book, she casually remarked that she wanted to get her mother a miniature garden. I told her I'd love to make Grandma a garden and photograph it for the book. We combed through garden centers for accessories that reminded us of Grandma. She has an antique watering can collection, so of course we had to put some of those in the garden. She and my grandpa always had birdhouses and birdbaths. You can see one of each nestled among the plants in this miniature garden.

Even though this is an outdoor garden, I still used a few tender annual plants and herbs. That will give Grandma something to do each spring, picking out new colorful annuals to fill the tiny garden.

The style of this garden—a backyard setting—will also lend itself well to holiday decorating, something else my grandma's a pro at doing.

Materials

Unable to decide whether to use the blue furniture or the white while at the garden center, I brought home both. (The blue, of course, ended up as the inspiration for the Wild Wild West Garden.)

Accessories

Flower fence
Arbor
Terra cotta pots
Birdbath pick
Gazing ball pick
Bird's nest pick
Bird house pick
American flag on flagpole

Resin frog
Lantern on a pick
Patio furniture
Wheelbarrow
Watering cans
Large planting urns
Fairy-sized small gravel
Gardening angel
Preserved sheet moss

Container

This container is all wood and has drainage holes drilled into the bottom. It measures 16 inches by 16 inches and is 3 inches deep.

Arranging the plants and accessories in the container at the garden center helps ensure that you arrive home with just the right number of plants to fill the garden.

Plants

"Trees"

Rosmarinus officinalis, rosemary

"Shrubs"

Miniature hosta
Ajuga 'Chocolate Chips'
Sagina subulata, Scotch moss
Calibrachoa, Million Bells

"Groundcovers"

Thymus praecox 'Pseudolanuginosus', woolly thyme
Thymus praecox 'Coccineus', red creeping thyme
Muehlenbeckia axillaris 'Nana', maidenhair vine (also labeled wirevine)

Purple, green, and gray are the predominant colors of the plants in this garden. More interest is added to the garden with blue, yellow, and red accessories.

All of the plants in this container can take full to partial sun, including the miniature hosta. It's a good idea to protect the garden from full hot afternoon sun, though. Several of the groundcovers are from the Stepables line of plants. The maidenhair vine is hardy to zone 7. It is possible that it will have to be replaced after a hard winter, but that's okay, as they can grow fairly aggressively.

Potting Soil

Use regular potting soil for outdoor garden containers.

Grandma's Garden Step by Step

Care and Maintenance

This garden will grow best if it remains outside. The *Ajuga* and hosta flowers will have to be removed when they're done blooming. The thyme and Scotch moss will need to be trimmed to keep it "in bounds." Grandma will have to keep training the wirevine so that it grows over the trellis.

The rosemary might or might not make it through the winter and may have to be replaced in the spring. The purple-flowering calibrachoa will have to be replaced (with the same or different plant) in the spring.

As the plants grow, this container will need more water, just as any normal outdoor container garden would. If the plants look droopy, or the top inch of soil is dry, the container needs water.

1. Fill the container halfway with potting soil. Some of the plants are larger than others, and I find that it's easier not to fill the entire container to start, but to fill it part way, plant the largest plants, and then add more soil before planting plants with smaller rootballs.

2. After filling the container with soil, arrange the plants and main accessories again just to make sure that you know where you want to put everything. Start by planting the largest plant (the miniature hosta) first. Then place the arbor and plant the wirevine. From there, you'll be able to fill in the rest of the plants. You can see, from the design, that the arbor anchors one corner, while the rosemary stands tall in the other corner. Plants of varying heights are scattered in between.

3. Add the extra soil around larger plants and ensure that they're settled before planting the smaller plants. You can see the three woolly thyme plants staggered around the garden. This helps achieve the design element of repetition. Two plants will go behind and next to the arbor, while one will be planted across the garden from the arbor to lead the eye around the garden.

Tip: It's handy to have floral wire and wire clippers when working with metal fences (to shorten them) and vines (to tie the vine to the arbor or fence to start training it). Cut ¾-inch-long pieces of floral wire to use when anchoring the vine to the arbor.

4. Secure the vine to the arbor. Plant the vine on one side of the arbor. Then, using bits of wire, tie pieces of vine to the arbor to encourage it to grow. You will have to continuously wind and train the wirevine. Unlike some vines, it doesn't have wrapping tendrils to secure itself to the arbor.

5. Pour the patio. I used fairy-sized gravel to make an informal gravel patio and pathway in the garden. This is where the patio set will sit and also where the wheelbarrow will rest.

6. Fill in around the plants with dried and preserved sheet moss. You can buy this moss, prepackaged, at a garden center or craft store. Don't use moss from your own garden unless you microwave it (for one minute on high) to kill any insects that might be living in it. Moss looks like a groundcover and adds green to the garden while the other groundcovers are just starting to grow and establish themselves.

7. "Plant" some moss in the miniature terra cotta pots to make the scene more lifelike.

8. Place the accessories. In a garden this large you can have several "scenes." There's a scene with the patio furniture under the arbor. A secondary "work area" showcases the wheelbarrow, small pots, and birdbath. In the corner by the rosemary there's a small bench and a bird "nesting" in the *Ajuga*.

Tell a Story with Accessories

Although you can certainly buy whatever looks cute and put it in your miniature garden, a garden will have so much more meaning if you select accessories that tell a story about you or the person for whom you're creating the garden.

Some gardens have fairies, but Grandma's Garden has a gardening angel. I selected this one because the yellow flowers added color to the garden.

Grandma and Grandpa always had a flagpole and flag in their front or back yard wherever they lived, so I had to include one in the miniature garden.

No matter how small the garden, Grandma always had an arbor or trellis with climbing roses, honeysuckle, black-eyed Susan vine, and hummingbird vines growing on it.

Garden under the Sea

To me, succulents have always looked like sea creatures or sea plants. This garden would be equally beautiful with a few more succulents and no accessories other than the blue tumbled glass mulch, but when you add a ceramic starfish, some shells, and a sea turtle, you create what's clearly an underwater world.

Most succulents will grow best in full to partial sun. Place this on a table in your porch or on the patio. It will become a conversation piece the moment your guests lay eyes on it.

Choose succulents that are hardy in your area for this style of garden.

Materials

The sea turtle and seal figurines are actually porcelain striker Wade figurines from Red Rose Tea tins. You can find these at flea markets and yard sales. You'll know that's what you're holding if the bottom is rough enough to strike a match against it.

A variety of hardy succulents

Accessories
Tumbled glass mulch
Sea shells
Sea animal figurines
Pottery sculpture

Container

A plain terra cotta azalea pot that's 12 inches in diameter and 6 inches deep.

Potting Soil
Use a mixture of two parts potting soil to one part vermiculite for this succulent dish garden.

Plants
The plants in the Garden under the Sea are all succulents hardy to zone 8. This includes some aloes, *Sempervivum* (hens and chickens), sedum, and other succulents. The exact plant list does not matter if you want to create this look. What *does* matter are the colors and shapes of the plants you select. When I purchased plants for this garden, my shopping list looked something like this:

One red succulent
One trailing sedum
Two medium-sized spiky succulents
One succulent that looks like brain coral

Not too specific, right?

Select plants that have the same sunlight requirements and that will contrast with one another in terms of form, size, color, and texture. Your Garden under the Sea won't look the same as this one, but it will have the same feel, and that's what you're going for.

Garden under the Sea
Step by Step

1. Fill the container with soil, leaving 2 inches between the soil line and the top of the container. Break apart any plants that you want to use in smaller clumps and in multiple places. Certain succulents aren't multi-stemmed, and can't be broken up. *Sedum* and *Sempervivum* are always good candidates for splitting, though.

2. Plant the plants. In this garden, one pot of *Sempervivum* has been split into several pieces, flanking the large succulent on the right side of the pot. I repeat—*repetition is your friend.*

3. Add height with long-stemmed succulents. I had these ghost plants (*Graptopetalum* spp.) growing in my garden. They were getting a little long on the stem and needed to be cut off and replanted in the garden to root closer to the ground, anyway. So I broke off a couple of pieces to stick into the Garden under the Sea to add height. You could just as easily achieve this effect with jade plants that have their lower leaves removed.

4. Topdress with mulch. Tumbled blue glass symbolizes water around these low-water plants. You can find tumbled glass at craft stores.

Tip: Sprinkling a few pieces of lighter blue glass on top of the darker glass mulch adds more depth to the garden. (Pun intended.)

5. Add accessories. The sea turtle figurine and ceramic starfish made the final cut. The gigantic painted koi fish did not. It just looked out of scale with the other plants and accessories.

Care and Maintenance

Remove the air plant once a week and run it under water to water it (unless it has rained during the week).

Periodically check around the base of the stems of each plant to make sure they aren't rotting. If you've had a lot of rain, you might want to move this garden under cover for a couple of weeks so that it can dry out a bit.

Water this garden when the leaves of the plants start to look less shiny or shrivel slightly. It's better to underwater succulents than to overwater them.

Air Plants + Succulents = Good Combination

Air plants and succulents grow well together. Air plants can be easily removed and watered under the sink, and, because they're not planted in the soil with the other plants, their water habits won't disrupt the succulents.

Make a hermit crab by placing an air plant inside a conch or snail shell.

I personalized this garden with a replica of my standup paddleboard and paddle "floating" over the Garden under the Sea. Gardening and paddling—two of my favorite things combined in one little scene.

You can customize with shells you've picked up on vacation or plants that look like the coral reefs you've snorkeled through. If you have an aquarium, you could paint ceramic figurines that look like your fish.

Tired of scrubbing out the birdbath? Plant a miniature water garden in it.

Miniature Water Garden

The curse of good drainage in a full-sized garden is that it's difficult to grow interesting sedges and rushes that need wet feet. You can still enjoy these plants without a hike to the swamp by planting a miniature water garden. By planting it in a birdbath, you can more easily enjoy the unique shapes and forms of the plants.

Plant what's available and hardy in your area, and whatever has a relatively small and shallow root system. Birdbaths aren't very deep.

Materials

The focus of this garden is the plants, not the accessories; however, a bunny in a little canoe wouldn't be out of place.

All of the plants used in this garden like to have "wet feet."

Accessories
Pea gravel is used as mulch around the plants to keep the soil in place.

Plants
Plants, clockwise from top left:

Cyperus prolifer, dwarf papyrus
Juncus filiformis 'Spiralis', Corkscrew rush
Acorus gramineus 'Aureopusillus Minimus', miniature variegated sweetflag
Adiantum spp., maidenhair fern

Container
A concrete birdbath on a pedestal or any shallow container without drainage will work.

Potting Soil
The plants are planted in playground sand as it's heavy and less likely to wash out.

Miniature Water Garden
Step by Step

1. Fill the birdbath with sand. Playground sand is certain to be clean and uniform.

2. Break up plants that you want to use in multiple pieces. Breaking up the plants helps reduce the size of their rootballs, thus allowing them to more easily settle into the shallow birdbath container.

Care and Maintenance

This garden needs virtually no maintenance other than watering. Make sure that the plants stay watered if you don't get rain for more than a week.

Some of the plants are hardier than others. After winter is over, take stock of what has returned for the season and what hasn't and replant. Replanting is a good excuse to try new water plants.

4. Topdress the garden with pebbles. Add pebbles until the sand is covered. The rocks will help keep the sand from running out when it rains and will help hold the plants upright.

3. Plant the plants. You can break up the rootballs and spread them out horizontally in the birdbath. Cover the roots with sand. Sand does not have the same amount of nutrients that soil would, but by allowing the water to collect in the garden (along with leaves and stray bits of plant debris that falls into it), the plants will receive nutrients.

5. Water the garden until water spills out over the sides of the birdbath.

This outdoor fairy garden is ready for a tea party.

Victorian Garden Party

Who doesn't love a tea party? When starting out as a miniature gardener or fairy gardener, some of the easiest accessories to find are those that will help you recreate a garden party, tea for two, or another semiformal outdoor setting. From pergolas to trellises, white-painted wrought-iron bistro tables and decorative miniature garden planting urns, you'll find hundreds of treasures in this style.

This project would work equally well as an outdoor or indoor mini-garden, depending on the plant choices. You can use a pergola or trellis as a focal point or unifying feature or a (relatively) larger shrub or plant as a "tree" in place of the pergola.

Think "white wicker" or "wrought iron" for your Victorian Garden Party miniature garden. Look for faux concrete urns and a tea set or lemonade pitcher. Ask yourself, "Would lovely ladies in white dresses like to sit a spell at this table or rest a minute on this bench?" It helps to put yourself in the place of the miniature inhabitants for whom you're planting the garden.

Materials

Accessories

White painted "wrought-iron" furniture, including
a pergola
Tiny gravel for a patio
"Concrete" birdbath and planting urns
Tea set
Birdhouse
Garden cloches
Topiary planter
Garden fairy

Container

The accessories used in this garden are somewhat ornate,
so your best container choices will be simple. A wide-
mouthed terra cotta bowl, a square miniature garden
planter, or a plain, glazed pot are all good containers for
this project.

Potting Soil

Use standard potting soil (not garden soil or topsoil) for
this project.

Plants

Because the accessories are key to this garden, choose
plants that will set off the accessories nicely. Remember
the principles of contrast (so that all of the plants and
accessories show up distinctly and don't blend together)
and scale (so that everything works together and creates a
lifelike scene), which you can see in the photo on the left.

You might not use every plant that you gather. That's
okay. You'll have more left for another garden, or because
these are outdoor plants, you can find a place to tuck
extras in the perennial border or give them away to
friends. I find it easier to have more choices, rather than
fewer, especially if I'm at home planting the garden, rather
than at the garden center.

"Trees"
Buxus spp., boxwood
Ilex vomitoria 'Nana', dwarf yaupon holly

"Shrubs"
Hosta 'Blue Mouse Ears', dwarf hosta
Ajuga 'Chocolate Chips'
Ophiopogon japonicus 'Nana', dwarf mondo grass

"Groundcovers"
Muehlenbeckia axillaris, wirevine (this is hardy where I
    live; it is an indoor plant in zones 6 and lower)
Mentha requienii, Corsican mint
Laurentia, white star creeper
Selaginella kraussiana 'Gold Tips', Gold Tips spikemoss
Ficus pumila var. *quercifolia*, oak leaf fig

Victorian Garden Party Step by Step

Care and Maintenance

Water this miniature garden as you'd water any other container garden: when the top inch of soil is dry.

The groundcovers planted in this garden can be aggressive. Keep the scissors handy to give the white star creeper a trim if it starts invading the space of the *Ajuga* or dwarf mondo grass.

Deadhead the *Ajuga* flowers (snip them with scissors) once they're finished blooming.

1. Fill the container. Add potting soil (not garden soil) to the container until it is one-half to two-thirds full. You want to leave room for the plants and still have a slight lip or edge of the pot sticking up when you're done planting and filling with soil. (That way, when you water the garden, you won't end up with soil or gravel spilling over the sides.)

2. Position the pergola. You always should position the largest plant or accessory first. If you were going to use a larger "tree" instead of a pergola, you'd place the tree first.

3. Break up your plants. One standard-sized pot of dwarf mondo grass or white star creeper goes a long way in a mini-garden. Separate plant clumps when you can in order to get more plants. You'll get more out of your purchases and you'll be able to mold the plantings to your design aesthetic, meaning you won't be stuck with large masses when smaller pieces would fit better.

4. Add accent plants. Once the massed plantings are in place (the mondo grass and white star creeper), you can add accent plants. In this planter, the oak leaf fig will trail over the side. The *Ajuga* is used as a specimen shrub in several places in the container. It is situated between the white star creeper and where the patio gravel will eventually go because its dark leaves will contrast against the lighter colored gravel.

Keep Adding to Your Miniature Garden

Just because the main assembly is done, the fun doesn't stop. I'm always on the prowl for accessories that will complete the look. In this case, I found some blown-glass "picks" to add to the garden that remind me of full-sized blown-glass art by one of my favorite artists, Barbara Sanderson. With their addition, this mini-garden is truly a little replica of my larger garden. (I also added a blown-glass marble to the birdbath to approximate the pond floats I have from Barbara.)

5. Add more potting soil. If you've primarily just positioned your plants, it's important to go back and actually plant them before you add accessories. You'll find out quickly, in a day or two, if you didn't plant something, as it will start to shrivel up because its roots are exposed to air and can't get water.

6. Create the patio. After the plants are planted and before you place the furniture and accessories, create the patio. I've used tiny gravel that mimics river rock. You could also use aquarium gravel. The smaller the pieces, the more it looks like pea gravel and less like a flagstone path or patio.

7. Position the accessories. Once the plants are all planted, you can add the accessories. Place the furniture, "plant" any miniature containers within the mini-garden, and set the table for tea. In this garden, tumbled blue glass serves as "water" in the birdbath. The finished garden is a perfect setting for a visiting garden fairy.

Design Alternatives
This garden would be just as charming without the pergola or with a tree as a focal point, or "shelter" under which the bistro set could be placed. If you were going to plant this garden with indoor plants, you could use ferns and polka-dot plants for the shrubs instead of the dwarf mondo grass and *Ajuga*. Use the spikemoss instead of the white star creeper for the groundcover. A dwarf myrtle or fig tree would work instead of a holly or boxwood if you want to include a tree instead of a pergola.

Same furniture, different garden. This miniature fairy garden has a small tree to provide shade or shelter over the same bistro table and chairs.

Soothing green and gray tones in the plants, container, and accessories make this garden restful to look at.

Botanical Garden

Miniature conifers are the showpiece plants of the Botanical Garden. True miniature conifers can be hard to find. Look for them at your local independent garden center. They can also be tricky to grow; however, if you can purchase them locally or buy them online, they're worth a try to grow because they are just so interesting. True mini-conifers grow less than 4 inches per year. (Some grow as little as ½ inch per year.) Yet they still look just like their full-sized counterparts. You'll have a, "Honey, I shrunk the plants!" reaction upon looking at them.

This is a garden designed and planted to last for a long time. It's worth the money to invest in a high-quality container (hypertufa, in this case) to showcase your tiny specimens. Unlike some of the other miniature gardens, with the right care, this garden can remain, virtually untouched, for several years.

Materials

To replicate the look of a botanical garden, use a variety of mulches and gravels for the patios and pathways. This gives the illusion of a garden that's larger, with different garden "rooms."

Clockwise, from lower left: alabaster chips, small fir bark pieces, and fairy garden gravel.

Plant a few perennials with the conifers for texture and depth.

Plants

Sedum, fine leaf gold stonecrop
Chamaecyparis obtusa 'Golden Sprite' (in finished garden), dwarf Hinoki cypress
Thuja occidentalis 'Golden Tuffet' (pictured), golden tuffet arborvitae
Miniature hosta
Juniperus horizontalis 'Pancake', dwarf creeping juniper
Chamaecyparis thyoides 'Red Star', dwarf white cedar
Ophiopogon japonicus 'Nanus', dwarf mondo grass (not pictured)

Accessories

"Concrete" fountain
"Concrete" statue
"White marble" resin statue
"Concrete" planting urn
Resin cat

The style of this garden is "formal historical" and is carried through with the faux concrete and marble accessories.

Hypertufa pots are handmade from a unique mixture of cement, peat moss, and perlite. As such, they have natural variations in color and texture.

Container

To complement the accessories, this garden is planted in a hypertufa pot that is 19 inches wide and 9 inches deep. While lighter than concrete, this container is still quite heavy when it's planted.

Potting Soil

Use regular potting soil for this project.

Botanical Garden
Step by Step

2. While you're placing the plants, you can also place the main accessories. In this garden, the biggest plant is the dwarf white cedar and the largest accessory is the fountain. (To give the fountain more width and height, it is placed on top of the base that came with the faux concrete statue.)

1. Fill the container with potting soil, leaving 3 inches between the top of the soil and the rim of the container. Place the plants in the pot to determine spacing. These plants are going to grow in the same pot for a long time, so this step is important. Plant them where you want them the first time. Take care to add soil so that all of the plants' roots are fully covered. (Dwarf mondo grass, in particular, resists being thoroughly planted. It seems like there's always a root that wants to escape. It is also a plant that doesn't grow well unless the roots are fully covered, unlike many succulents.)

3. Mulch the garden. White alabaster chips form a base for one of the statues. Fine granite chip gravel (which came as mulch on top of the miniature conifers) covers the "ground" around the concrete fountain and "marble" statue. Small fir bark chips act as "regular" wood mulch, like what you'd see around the plants in the flower beds at a botanical garden.

Tip: Don't leave the soil bare! You can always use small wood-chip mulch or soil conditioner as mulch on top of a miniature garden.

4. Place the accessories. This statue did not have a pick on the bottom side. It is propped in the garden with alabaster chips at the base to hold it up. The white rock chips contrast nicely with the dark gray of the statue.

What Is Unique?

When thinking about accessories for any garden's theme, try to remember what makes the place that you're recreating with plants different than anywhere else. What is unique about the scene that you're building?

This miniature botanical garden has a cat resting on the pathway just like many "real" life-sized botanical gardens do. Cats are an important part of the integrated pest-management program at Longwood Gardens where I went to school. Each garden area has its own cat that is responsible for "small mammal population control." If there's a garden near you, think about what makes it unique and special, and recreate some of that in miniature for your tabletop version.

Every garden needs a cat.

Is this a full-sized statue in a large garden or a miniature statue in a miniature garden? When you pay careful attention to scale, you can create tiny lifelike worlds ready for exploring.

167

What a fun surprise to stumble across this fairy hideaway in the middle of a life-sized garden!

Woodland Hideaway

Fairy gardens in the middle of life-sized gardens are a delightful surprise for garden visitors young and old. You can create an *in situ* (in place) fairy garden or miniature garden with any theme you can dream up. These larger mini-gardens are ideal for showcasing collections of plants or for setting up larger furniture and accessories. Do you have an outdoor train set? Make a miniature garden around it to provide more for the train's passengers to see.

This miniature garden is a woodland hideaway suited for fairies of all shapes and sizes. It even includes a lifelike campfire with marshmallow roasting sticks.

Materials

A bigger garden means more room for accessories.

Accessories
Rustic wood bench
Clay or plastic mushrooms
White picket fence
Flag and flagpole
"No Humans Allowed" sign
Wheelbarrow
Clothesline
Fairy house
Resin rabbit
Garden tools
Campfire and marshmallows
Birdbath
Basket
Watering can
Bucket
Stone mat

Container
There is no container for this garden. It was planted in the middle of a larger garden in an area that is mostly shaded with a couple of hours of midmorning sun.

Plants
Fuchsia spp., fuchsia
Heuchera spp., coral bells
Abutilon spp., flowering maple
Pteris spp., table fern
Ophiopogon japonicus 'Nanus', dwarf mondo grass
Ajuga 'Chocolate Chips'
Hosta 'Blue Mouse Ears' (not pictured)
Buxus spp., miniature boxwood

This empty space will soon be a fairy garden!

Woodland Hideaway
Step by Step

1. Prepare the area for the miniature garden by digging some potting soil into the area where you plan to plant.

2. Place the largest plant or accessory, in this case the fairy house. It will serve as a focal point and anchor, around which you will build the rest of the garden.

3. Create the pathway by removing the steppingstones from the mat and placing them individually in the garden.

4. Place the plants. In this garden, they form a horseshoe shape around the fairy house and the patio or pathway.

5. Plant the plants, taking care to make sure they are fully planted at the correct depth. (The soil line of the garden is even with the soil line of the plants' rootballs.)

6 . Place the accessories. Because this is an outdoor garden, ceramic, wood, or plastic accessories work best. Water the garden. You can water outdoor miniature and fairy gardens with the same frequency that you'd water other outdoor annual and perennial gardens.

Creating Scenes Within a Scene

More space means more room to play. The Woodland Hideaway has several places for fairies to relax, including a campfire, the fairy house, and the rustic garden bench in the shade of a miniature hosta.

The campfire, including a stack of firewood, log benches, marshmallow sticks, and the fire pit, were handmade by an artist on Etsy.

A second seating area composed of a garden bench situated between a fuchsia plant and a miniature hosta is completed with a handmade ceramic birdbath and a resin bunny rabbit keeping watch.

Part 3
PLANT PROFILES

This section includes commonly available plants that are well-suited to miniature gardens, fairy gardens, and terrariums. They are loosely organized by type: indoor/outdoor plants, succulents, and miniature conifers. There are many other choices beyond the plants listed, however. Whenever you visit the garden center, take a look around and scout for plants for your next creation. If you're willing to put a little bit more time into maintenance of the garden, you can use groundcovers that might need more frequent trimming or an annual flower that will have to be replaced each season.

The Diamond Frost™ euphorbia is an annual that has to be replaced every year, while the *Hosta* 'Blue Mouse Ears' (left) is a perennial that will come back each spring. The flowers of the 'Diamond Frost' are so airy and fairy-like that it's worth a few dollars to replace it yearly just to be able to enjoy it during the summer.

Don't ignore the perennials section of the garden center. You might find a miniature like this hosta lurking in a back corner, waiting to be taken home and planted.

Varying forms and textures make this an eye-catching plant combination. *Clockwise from top: Eugenia myrtifolia 'Nanum',* Teenie Genie® Miniature Brush Cherry, *Ficus pumila* var. quercifolia, *Hypoestes phyllostachya,* Green and white polka dot plant.

Plant Profiles

The main things to keep in mind when shopping for plants are:

- Light and water requirements: It's helpful if all of the plants in one garden have the *same* light and water requirements.

- Growth rate: A faster growth rate equals more maintenance (in terms of trimming and, possibly, replanting).

- Contrasting form, color, and texture: Contrast is what will make your miniature garden interesting.

Get the look of popular full-sized garden giant blue hostas with the small stature of miniature *Hosta* 'Blue Mouse Ears'.

This small tree provides a big burst of bright color in the miniature garden.

Miniature Hosta
Hosta 'Blue Mouse Ears'

Garden type:	**outdoor**
Use/function:	**tree, shrub**
Hardiness zone:	**3–9**
Height:	**5 inches**
Growth rate:	**slow**
Light:	**shade to part shade**
Water needs:	**low to medium**

Miniature hostas are a must for the outdoor fairy and miniature garden. They come in different shapes and sizes, but 'Blue Mouse Ears' is one of the easiest miniature hostas to find in garden centers and online. This shrunken version of a staple of full-sized gardens can be used as a shrub or tree in the miniature garden. The leaves, when paired with the right accessories, look like giant tropical elephant ears. Look for other miniature hosta varieties for your outdoor gardens.

Wilma Goldcrest (Monterey) Cypress
Cupressus macrocarpa 'Wilma Goldcrest'

Garden type:	**outdoor, indoor**
Use/function:	**tree**
Hardiness zone:	**7–10**
Height:	**varies**
	(8–16 inches is common)
Growth rate:	**slow**
Light:	**full sun to part sun**
Water needs:	**low to medium**

The chartreuse foliage of this slow-growing evergreen creates eye-popping contrast in the miniature landscape. Because of its size and columnar form, it makes a good tree or focal point. If left outside, this plant will grow to a mature height of 8 feet (but that takes up to twenty years). It can be used for indoor gardens in all regions and outdoor gardens in warmer areas. It's drought-tolerant when it becomes established.

Teenie Genie™ can be trained as a standard or topiary tree in the miniature garden.

Diamond Frost® looks like it was created specifically to grow in fairy gardens.

Table ferns are a group of small ferns that grow well indoors.

Teenie Genie™ Miniature Brush Cherry *Eugenia myrtifolia* 'Nanum'

Garden type:	**outdoor, indoor**
Use/function:	**tree**
Hardiness zone:	**9–11 (grows well outside in summer; can be brought inside in winter)**
Height:	**varies (6–12 inches is common)**
Growth rate:	**very slow**
Light:	**full sun to part shade**
Water needs:	**medium to high**

Looking for the perfect little topiary tree for your mini-garden? *Eugenia* is a great choice. These are evergreen shrubs that are hardy outside only in the warmest areas, but they will grow outside during the summer and inside year-round. They need bright light, so if you're planting them as part of an indoor garden, plan to keep the garden next to a west- or south-facing window.

Diamond Frost™ Euphorbia *Euphorbia graminea* 'Diamond Frost'

Garden type:	**outdoor/indoor**
Use/function:	**tree, flowers**
Hardiness zone:	**9–10 (mostly grown as an annual)**
Height:	**8–12 inches**
Growth rate:	**fast**
Light:	**full sun to part sun**
Water needs:	**medium**

Diamond Frost™ is one of the most popular annual plants ever developed. It hit the market in 2005, and gardeners have been loving it ever since. It's easy to care for, drought-tolerant, and blooms without deadheading. It grows best outside or indoors in a bright window. While I don't usually think of annuals as a fairy garden plant, the floaty, airy quality of this plant's growth and blooms makes it work well in a miniature or fairy garden.

Table Ferns *Pteris* spp.

Garden type:	**indoor**
Use/function:	**shrub**
Hardiness zone:	**n/a**
Height:	**2–4 inches**
Growth rate:	**slow**
Light:	**low to medium**
Water needs:	**medium (soil should stay moist but not soggy)**

Not all ferns grow well inside, as anyone who has tried to bring a big Boston fern inside for the winter knows. Many outdoor ferns are messy, drop leaves, and are too big for a miniature garden. Table ferns, *Pteris* spp., thrive in lower light, can live with lower humidity (but still grow well in terrariums), and don't drop their leaves. Look for plants with different leaf shapes, colors, and textures to add variety to miniature gardens.

Plant Profiles

Variegated coral bells brighten up a shady outdoor garden.

The purple flowers of *Ajuga* in the spring add interest to every miniature garden.

Cute and culinary, rosemary is a double-duty miniature garden plant.

Coral Bells
Heuchera spp.

Garden type:	**outdoor**
Use/function:	**shrub**
Hardiness zone:	**4–9, but can vary with cultivar**
Height:	**varies (between 3–10 inches)**
Growth rate:	**slow**
Light:	**shade to part shade**
Water needs:	**medium**

You can plant any coral bells (also commonly referred to by its Latin name, *Heuchera*) cultivars in your miniature gardens, but some grow to be large and will have to be replaced. If you want to keep a perennial heuchera in the garden for several years, look for the Little Cutie™ series of *Heuchera*. 'Coco' is a burgundy-leafed variety, 'Sweet Tart' has chartreuse leaves, and 'Sugar Berry' has purplish pink leaves with dark veins. These miniature coral bells will grow to be no larger than 6 inches tall.

Bugleweed
Ajuga 'Chocolate Chips'

Garden type:	**outdoor**
Use/function:	**shrub, groundcover**
Hardiness zone:	**4–9**
Height:	**4 inches**
Growth rate:	**medium**
Light:	**full sun to partial shade**
Water needs:	**medium**

'Chocolate Chips' is a smaller-leafed variety of *Ajuga* than the species. It is absolutely perfect for outdoor miniature gardens. Although it is a groundcover, it spreads fairly slowly, and as such requires less trimming and maintenance than other groundcovers. Usually you can separate one 4-inch or quart pot into smaller clumps, getting more bang for your buck at the garden center.

Rosemary
Rosmarinus officinalis

Garden type:	**indoor/outdoor**
Use/function:	**tree**
Hardiness zone:	**7–10**
Height:	**can grow to be 3 feet tall (requires pruning)**
Growth rate:	**medium**
Light:	**full sun**
Water needs:	**low**

Rosemary makes an excellent tree for a miniature garden if you're willing to prune it. The good thing about pruning rosemary, though, is that the trimmings have great use in the kitchen. You can leave rosemary outside if you live in zone 7 or higher. (It is marginally hardy in zone 6.) Look for upright varieties if you want to use it as a tree. Rosemary doesn't like to be overwatered. Take care to let the soil dry out between waterings.

Easy to grow and prehistoric-looking, *Peperomia* is a perfect terrarium plant.

Polka dot plants come in a variety of colors and variegations, from white and green, to red and white, to pink and green.

The flowers of fuchsia plants add color to the miniature garden.

Ripple Peperomia
Peperomia caperata

Garden type:	**indoor/terrarium**
Use/function:	**shrub**
Hardiness zone:	**n/a**
Height:	**up to 6 inches**
Growth rate:	**slow**
Light:	**medium**
Water needs:	**high**

Peperomia is a common houseplant that grows well in terrariums and dish gardens. It has a medium- to low-light requirement and thrives in moderately moist soil. Start with 1-inch plants when planting in terrariums. This species of *Peperomia* comes in a variety of colors, though burgundy is the most common.

Polka Dot Plant
Hypoestes phyllostachya

Garden type:	**indoor/terrarium**
Use/function:	**shrub**
Hardiness zone:	**9–10**
Height:	**up to 8 inches; can be maintained with pruning**
Growth rate:	**medium**
Light:	**medium**
Water needs:	**medium**

Polka dot plants are a staple of every terrarium planting because they add color to what can sometimes be a predominantly green color palette. Look for polka dot plants in the houseplant and outdoor plant sections of nurseries or even large chain stores, which often carry plants. Larger clumps can be separated into smaller pieces for use in dish gardens. You can prune this plant to maintain its size at under 4 inches.

Fuchsia
Fuchsia spp.

Garden type:	**outdoor**
Use/function:	**tree**
Hardiness zone:	**n/a (grown as an annual)**
Height:	**up to 2 feet**
Growth rate:	**depends on the species**
Light:	**part shade to full shade**
Water needs:	**medium**

There *are* some hardy miniature fuchsias that grow in zones 7–10, but they can be difficult to find. If you want to add some fairy flowers to the garden, grab a fuchsia plant in a 4-inch pot and enjoy it in the outdoor garden throughout the summer. You'll have to replant next year, but the beautiful flower colors are worth the trouble.

Plant Profiles

Flowering maples bloom all summer.

No other plant for the miniature garden has the same grasslike form as the dwarf mondo grass.

Arrowhead plants need low light and high moisture, so they're excellent terrarium plants.

Flowering Maple
Abutilon x *hybridum*

Garden type:	**outdoor**
Use/function:	**tree**
Hardiness zone:	**n/a**
Height:	**up to 2 feet; can be maintained to 8 inches with pruning**
Growth rate:	**medium**
Light:	**full sun to part shade**
Water needs:	**medium**

The blooms of the annual flowering maple (which is no relation to maple trees; they're actually in the hibiscus family) look like little fairy hats, so they're a must-grow plant for outdoor fairy gardens. They are annuals that will have to be replaced yearly. You can find flowering maples with blooms in shades of yellow, red, pink, peach, and orange.

Dwarf Mondo Grass
Ophiopogon japonicus 'Nanus'

Garden type:	**outdoor (but you can cheat and use it for indoor gardens)**
Use/function:	**groundcover, ornamental grass**
Hardiness zone:	**6–11**
Height:	**3 inches**
Growth rate:	**slow**
Light:	**part sun**
Water needs:	**consistently moist**

Dwarf mondo grass provides texture in the garden that no other plant can offer. It isn't a true grass, but it's the closest thing to grass that will grow in a miniature garden. The narrow, straplike leaves contrast with every other plant form. Use this for borders in a miniature garden, as ornamental grasses, or as shrubs in the garden. In larger, in-ground gardens, dwarf mondo grass can serve as a groundcover.

Arrowhead Plant
Syngonium podophyllum

Garden type:	**indoor/terrarium**
Use/function:	**shrub, tree (if using accessories less than 1 inch tall)**
Hardiness zone:	**n/a**
Height:	**can grow to 6 inches**
Growth rate:	**medium**
Light:	**low**
Water needs:	**high**

Arrowhead plants are commonly found in the "tiny plant" sections of garden centers. Some varieties can grow to be large, but if you can locate plants in 1-inch pots, they'll remain small enough for terrariums and dish gardens for a few years. Look for plants with different colors and variegation patterns on the leaves to add variety.

A variegated ficus has built-in color contrast between the green leaf centers and white leaf margins (edges).

Croton plants have bright and colorful leaves.

Skinny chartreuse leaves of this *Alternanthera* plant add color and texture contrast in the miniature garden.

Ficus Tree
Ficus benjamina

Garden type: **indoor/terrarium**
Use/function: **tree**
Hardiness zone: **10**
Height: **can grow up to 50 feet tall outside (but won't get that tall inside; can be pruned)**
Growth rate: **slow**
Light: **medium to bright indoor light**
Water needs: **medium**

Ficus benjamina plants are popular for interiorscaping at shopping malls and offices. They make excellent houseplants but are fussy about being moved. Once you find a place where a ficus is happy growing, *leave it alone*. If you have to move it, be patient, as it might drop its leaves. Give it a few weeks to regrow before you decide to remove it and plant a new one.

Croton
Croton spp.

Garden type: **indoor/terrarium**
Use/function: **tree, shrub**
Hardiness zone: **10**
Height: **can grow to be large or be pruned to maintain smaller height**
Growth rate: **slow**
Light: **bright indirect light**
Water needs: **medium (let soil dry out before watering)**

Crotons are easy-care plants, but if they're repotted or moved, they will sometimes drop their leaves. Not to worry, they'll grow back in a few weeks. Look for plants in 1-inch pots for terrariums. Crotons in 2-inch or 4-inch pots will still be small enough for larger miniature gardens. You can find these plants with leaves that are spotted, striped, and different colors, including pink, yellow, red, orange, and green.

Joseph's Coat
Alternanthera 'Thingold'

Garden type: **indoor/terrarium**
Use/function: **shrub**
Hardiness zone: **n/a**
Height: **5 inches**
Growth rate: **slow**
Light: **bright**
Water needs: **medium**

The multicolored leaves of *Alternanthera* plants make them good choices when you need something besides straight green in the garden. This variety has thin chartreuse leaves, but you can find *Alternanthera* plants with red, orange, pink, and purple leaves too. It needs bright light to grow, so use it in miniature gardens and terrariums that will be placed beside a window. 'Thingold' is a cultivar especially suited for miniature gardens because of its thin leaves and chartreuse color that contrasts with other, darker-leafed plants. It also grows well in terrariums.

Plant Profiles

White flowers on white star creeper open throughout the summer.

Spikemoss looks like a cross between a fern and a moss.

Aloe isn't just for the first-aid kit.

White Star Creeper
Laurentia fluviatilis

Garden type:	**outdoor**
Use/function:	**groundcover**
Hardiness zone:	**7–9**
Height:	**3 inches**
Growth rate:	**fast**
Light:	**partial shade**
Water needs:	**medium**

White star creeper is a somewhat aggressive groundcover that grows well in partial shade. Plant this in your miniature garden if you want to do more maintenance—in terms of trimming—to keep this plant from taking over. The tradeoff for time spent caring for the plant is that it blooms almost continuously for several months. It is happiest when kept moist; you'll see a new flush of bloom after you water it.

Gold Spikemoss
Selaginella kraussiana 'Aurea'

Garden type:	**indoor/terrarium/ outdoor**
Use/function:	**groundcover**
Hardiness zone:	**zone 6**
Height:	**4 inches**
Growth rate:	**medium**
Light:	**partial to full shade, bright indirect light indoors**
Water needs:	**high**

Spikemoss can be temperamental, but it's worth a try to grow, as nothing else has the same soft, fluffy form and low growth habit. The key to success is plenty of water and humidity. It grows well in terrariums, but it can sometimes rot if it's kept too wet. If using in an outdoor garden, group with partial-sun to full-shade plants. It doesn't tolerate full, hot sun all day.

Aloe
Aloe spp.

Garden type:	**indoor/outdoor/ succulent**
Use/function:	**tree or shrub, depending on size**
Hardiness zone:	**varies with species (grown as an indoor plant in zones 6 and lower)**
Height:	**up to 1 foot**
Growth rate:	**slow**
Light:	**high bright light when indoors**
Water needs:	**low**

Aloe plants grow best when planted with other low-water plants, including succulents. There are many species of aloe, some of which are larger than others. All grow well in miniature gardens for the first several years of their lives. You can't really prune aloes to contain their size, so when the plants get too large for a miniature garden, pot them up separately and give them to friends as gifts.

Haworthia plants look like tiny agaves and are at home in a desert or beach garden.

Hens and chickens reproduce like rabbits!

Jade plants are easy to grow as "trees" for western-themed gardens.

Haworthia
Haworthia **spp.**

Garden type:	**indoor**
Use/function:	**shrub/desert plant/ under-the-sea plant**
Hardiness zone:	**varies**
Height:	**varies**
Growth rate:	**slow**
Light:	**bright**
Water needs:	**low**

In the miniature garden, haworthia plants look much like century plants, which are huge agaves that can grow to be 6 or 7 feet tall. Use these low-water plants in your succulent garden. Their spiky upright form contrasts with the "roundy-moundy" form of many succulent plants. Compared to some succulents, they also grow well indoors and don't suffer from low-light situations.

Hens and Chickens
Sempervivum **spp.**

Garden type:	**outdoor/indoor**
Use/function:	**shrub**
Hardiness zone:	**varies**
Height:	**1–4 inches**
Growth rate:	**fast**
Light:	**bright**
Water needs:	**low**

I remember hens and chickens overflowing out of strawberry pots in my grandma's garden. Today, you can find these plants in shades of red, blue-gray, light green, and dark green. They do reproduce pretty quickly with new baby plants forming along the sides of the larger rosettes. You can break off these new plants to use in other miniature gardens. Plant hens and chickens with other succulents and low-water use plants.

Jade Plant
Crassula **spp.**

Garden type:	**indoor**
Use/function:	**tree, shrub (depending on the size and shape)**
Hardiness zone:	**n/a**
Height:	**can grow up to 4 or 5 feet tall, but can (and should) be kept the size you want it by pruning**
Growth rate:	**slow**
Light:	**bright, indirect light**
Water needs:	**low**

Jade plants come in many shapes and sizes. Some look like miniature trees, while others look like brain coral. *Crassula* 'Jitters' is used in the Garden under the Sea. It's the largest plant in the garden, but it looks nothing like the jade plant pictured here. Use jade plants in succulent gardens, but don't mix them with high-water-use plants.

Plant Profiles

Graptopetalum plants can grow into small "trees" in the mini-garden.

There is a wide variety of creeping sedum selections with leaf colors ranging from green to red to gray-blue.

Blue-gray leaves provide different color in the garden.

Ghost Plant
Graptopetalum spp.

Garden type: **indoor/outdoor**
Use/function: **tree, shrub**
Hardiness zone: **varies by species. If hardy to your area, they'll be located outdoors in the perennials area of a garden center.**
Height: **up to 8 inches; can be cut off and reset so that the rosette of leaves is closer to the ground**
Growth rate: **medium**
Light: **bright**
Water needs: **low, but can tolerate some humidity and heavy rains**

Graptopetalum plants form rosettes of leaves on ever-elongating stems. When the stems get too long, you can cut the plants off at the base of the leaves and reset the rosette on the soil. It's easy to propagate new plants. Just break off a leaf and stick it in the soil. A new plant will form at the base of the old leaf. Plant these with other low-water-use plants, though out of all of the succulents pictured, this one can take the most water.

Stonecrop, Creeping Sedum
Sedum spp.

Garden type: **outdoor/indoor**
Use/function: **groundcover, shrub**
Hardiness zone: **varies with species**
Height: **up to 6 inches**
Growth rate: **medium**
Light: **high**
Water needs: **low**

Creeping sedum plants have different growth habits than the common *Sedum* 'Autumn Joy' and other erect-type sedums that you see in full-sized gardens, which make them ideal for miniature gardens. Hardiness of these creeping types varies by species, so read the plant tag carefully if you plan to keep them outside. You can often split up a pot into several plant clumps, making these plants a good bang for the buck.

Friendship Plant
Pilea 'Aquamarine'

Garden type: **indoor/terrarium**
Use/function: **groundcover**
Hardiness zone: **n/a**
Height: **less than 1 inch**
Growth rate: **medium**
Light: **bright indirect**
Water needs: **medium**

Friendship plant has a succulent, fleshy leaf, but it tolerates lower light and humidity fairly well, so it is often used in terrariums as a groundcover. It's easy to grow and propagate. If you want more of it, just break off a piece from your current plant, stick it in soil, and let it root.

This small blooming plant looks like a grass, but it's not one.

Maidenhair vines are vigorous.

One parlor palm is actually several plants that can be split into smaller clumps.

Miniature Variegated Sweetflag
Acorus gramineus 'Aureopusillus Minimus'

Garden type: **outdoor/water garden**
Use/function: **shrub, ornamental grass**
Hardiness zone: **5–7**
Height: **up to 4 inches**
Growth rate: **slow**
Light: **partial sun**
Water needs: **high**

This grasslike plant is an excellent choice for miniature water gardens. Its long, thin, light green leaves provide excellent contrasting color and texture in any garden in which it's planted. It belongs with other water-loving plants, though.

Maidenhair Vine, Wirevine
Muehlenbeckia axillaris 'Nana'

Garden type: **indoor/outdoor/ terrarium**
Use/function: **groundcover, vine**
Hardiness zone: **5**
Height: **unlimited**
Growth rate: **fast**
Light: **partial shade**
Water needs: **medium**

Wirevine is in almost every fairy garden that has an arbor in it. This vine is easy to grow and can be used either as a groundcover or a climber. It does not like to dry out, though, and will shrivel up quickly if the roots aren't kept evenly moist. Feel free to prune and trim to your heart's content. It will just grow back.

Parlor Palm
Chamaedorea elegans

Garden type: **indoor/terrarium**
Use/function: **tree**
Hardiness zone: **n/a**
Height: **6–12 inches**
Growth rate: **slow**
Light: **bright**
Water needs: **medium**

Parlor palms are champion houseplants. They can deal with low light and low humidity. These palms can grow up to 5 feet tall, but you can keep them smaller by cutting old stems down to the ground. They're happier with bright, indirect light, but they will tolerate artificial light. Use parlor palms with taller terrarium containers or in indoor miniature gardens.

Plant Profiles

It's an annual flower but one that looks right at home in the fairy garden.

With a growth rate of ¼ inch per year, this miniature conifer will stay small for a long time.

Golden Tuffet is a chartreuse-leafed miniature arborvitae with a round growing habit. Its leaves turn bronze in the fall.

Million Bells
Calibrachoa hybrids

Garden type:	**outdoor**
Use/function:	**shrub**
Hardiness zone:	**n/a**
Height:	**5 inches**
Growth rate:	**fast**
Light:	**full sun**
Water needs:	**medium**

Use million bells (also commonly called calibrachoa) in place of a shrub if you want to have a "flowering shrub" in the miniature garden. You don't have to deadhead these annuals, but you can trim them to keep them from growing out of bounds. They will have to be replanted every year.

Dwarf Hinoki Cyprus
Chamaecyparis obtusa 'Golden Sprite'

Garden type:	**outdoor**
Use/function:	**shrub**
Hardiness zone:	**5–8**
Height:	**1 foot by 1 foot after 10 years**
Growth rate:	**slow**
Light:	**full sun to partial shade**
Water needs:	**medium**

'Golden Sprite' is a true miniature conifer, growing less than 1 inch per year. It is perfect for outdoor miniature gardens that you plan to keep in the same container without repotting. Grow it with other dwarf and miniature conifers and perennials.

Golden Tuffet Arborvitae
Thuja occidentalis 'Golden Tuffet'

Garden type:	**outdoors**
Use/function:	**shrub**
Hardiness zone:	**3–8**
Height:	**12 to 24 inches**
Growth rate:	**slow**
Light:	**full to partial sun**
Water needs:	**medium—more in high heat or bright sun**

This is a dwarf arborvitae that adds interesting color to the miniature garden year-round. It grows well with other dwarf conifers and moderate water-use, full-sun perennials. If you have room for an outdoor in-situ garden, definitely order one of these plants for contrast and interest.

A larger dwarf "tree" for the outdoor miniature garden.

This dwarf creeping juniper is almost too cute for words.

Look for different shapes and sizes of air plants when shopping.

Dwarf White Cedar
Chamaecyparis thyoides 'Red Star'

Garden type:	**outdoor**
Use/function:	**tree**
Hardiness zone:	**4–8**
Height:	**at full maturity this tree can be large—up to 20 feet; however, it takes years to get that big.**
Growth rate:	**medium**
Light:	**full to partial sun**
Water needs:	**low once established**

Use the 'Red Star' white cedar as an anchor plant in your in-ground or larger permanent-container miniature garden. While small, this plant has the juvenile white cedar foliage—star-shaped leaves—as opposed to the "adult" straight needles. Once it has outgrown a container, you can plant it in the garden.

Dwarf Creeping Juniper
Juniperus horizontalis 'Pancake'

Garden type:	**outdoor**
Use/function:	**shrub, groundcover**
Hardiness zone:	**3–9**
Height:	**3–4 inches (and 2 feet wide)**
Growth rate:	**slow**
Light:	**full to partial sun**
Water needs:	**low once established**

'Pancake' dwarf creeping juniper looks so much like its larger counterparts that it's a perfect miniature garden plant. Few miniature plants provide the type of scale and grounding needed to create a realistic scene without accessories, but you can tell this one is a mini just by looking at it. Plant it in your permanent miniature gardens and containers.

Air Plant
Tillandsia spp.

Garden type:	**any garden as an accent; must be brought indoors in the winter**
Use/function:	**accents and highlights**
Hardiness zone:	**varies**
Height:	**varies**
Growth rate:	**slow**
Light:	**bright indirect**
Water needs:	**soak once a week or mist two or three times a week**

Air plants are so fun and unusual that I try to find ways to work them into "regular" miniature gardens. In the Wild Wild West Garden, they stood in for tumbling tumbleweeds. In the Garden under the Sea, I put the end of one in a conch shell to make a sea creature. They're easy to care for as long as you water them at least once a week. Regular garden centers are starting to carry more air plants, but you can also find them easily online for purchase.

Whew! After all of that garden design, this little gardening fairy is ready to relax in the garden and enjoy a cup of tea with her puppy by her side. Now it's your turn to get growing!

RESOURCES

There's information sprinkled throughout the book about where to get miniature garden plants, accessories, and containers. Before you order anything online, always visit your local garden center and craft store. You'll be surprised at what you can find.

Look in the floral arrangement department for moss, decorative stones, floral wire, and picks.

Pick up a hot glue gun and acrylic paints in the crafts section.

Check for dollhouse miniatures at craft stores, toy shops, and train stores.

Visit local art fairs, consignment shops, and flea markets to find figurines, interesting containers, and one-of-a-kind accessories.

Beyond local businesses, here are some places to find plants and accessories:

Etsy.com
Etsy is an online marketplace with one-of-a-kind accessories and hard-to-find plants.

Fairygardening.com
This website for one brand of fairy gardening accessories and plants has a "find a retailer location" search function.

Song Sparrow Nursery
www.songsparrow.com
This is a good online source for purchasing dwarf conifers.

Stepables
www.stepables.com
Stepables has information about and an online store for ordering short-statured groundcovers. They also have a retailer-locator function on the website.

If you want more information about plants for miniature gardens, try these resources:

Indoor Plants: The Essential Guide to Choosing and Caring for Houseplants
Jane Courtier and Graham Clarke
This book includes all houseplants, not necessarily just miniature plants, but has great information about how to care for indoor plants, which can be even trickier than caring for outdoor plants.

Planting Designs for Cactus and Succulents
Indoor and Outdoor Projects for Unique, Easy-Care Plants—In All Climates
Sharon Asakawa, John Bagnasco, Robyn M. Foreman, Shaun Buchanan
This book has information about selecting succulents for indoor and outdoor use, along with care tips.

American Conifer Society
www.conifersociety.org
This site has information and links about full-sized (but also about dwarf) conifers.

Index

Meet Katie Elzer-Peters

Katie Elzer-Peters has been gardening since she could walk, a hobby-turned-career nurtured by her parents and grandparents. After receiving a bachelor's degree in public horticulture from Purdue University, Katie completed the Longwood Graduate Program at Longwood Gardens and the University of Delaware, receiving a master's degree in public garden management.

Katie has served as a horticulturist, head of gardens, educational programs director, development officer, and manager of botanical gardens around the United States, including the Washington Park Arboretum in Seattle, Washington; the Indianapolis Zoo in Indianapolis, Indiana; the Marie Selby Botanical Garden in Sarasota, Florida; the Smithsonian Institution in Washington, D.C.; Longwood Gardens in Kennett Square, Pennsylvania; Winterthur Museum, Garden, and Library in Greenville, Delaware; the King's Garden at Fort Ticonderoga in Ticonderoga, New York; and Airlie Gardens in Wilmington, North Carolina.

Whether at a botanical garden, or for a garden center, garden club, or school group, Katie has shared her love of gardening by teaching classes and workshops, and writing brochures, articles, gardening website information, and columns. While serving as curator of landscape at Fort Ticonderoga, Katie planned and led garden bus tours along the east coasts of the United States and Canada.

Today, Katie lives and gardens with her husband and dogs, Lucy and Jack Daniels Elzer-Peters III, in the coastal city of Wilmington, North Carolina, (zone 8a). She has an enormous "in-ground" garden, including flowers and vegetables, and a fleet of miniature gardens too. Katie manages GreatGardenSpeakers.com, an online speaker directory of garden, design, ecology, and horticultural speakers. She also owns the Garden of Words, LLC, a marketing and PR firm specializing in garden-industry clients.

Katie is the author of the *Beginner's Illustrated Guide to Gardening: Techniques to Help You Get Started*, as well as five other books about vegetable gardening, all published by Cool Springs Press.